LEADERS LAB

Leaders Lab

66 Ways to Develop
Your Leadership
Skill, Strategy & Style

JANE MOYER

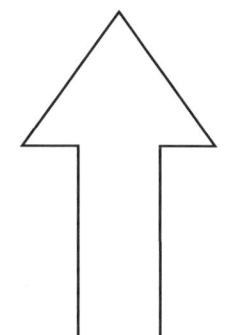

Copyright © New Century Leadership LLC 2016
All Rights Reserved.

No part of this publication may be reproduced, stored in a retrieval system, or transmitted by any means — electronic, mechanical, photocopy, recording, or otherwise — without prior permission in writing from the Publisher (except by a reviewer, who may quote brief passages in a review). Requests to the Publisher for permissions may be sent to publisher@newcenturyleadership.com.

Disclaimer: While the Publisher and Author have used their best efforts in preparing this book, they make no representations or warranties with respect to the accuracy or completeness of the contents of this work and specifically disclaim all warranties, including without limitation implied warranties of merchantability or fitness for a particular purpose. No warranty may be created or extended by sales or promotional materials. The advice and strategies contained herein may not be suitable for every situation. You should consult with a professional where appropriate. The Author and the Publisher disclaim any liability, loss, or risk resulting directly or indirectly from the use or application of any of the contents of this book, including but not limited to special, incidental, consequential, or other damages.

Published by New Century Leadership LLC, P.O. Box 223, Hinsdale IL 60522

Cover and graphic design by J-nett Asa.

Library of Congress Control Number: 2015919621

ISBN (paperback): 978-1-940975-04-7   (ebook) 978-1-940975-05-4

CONTENTS

Introduction: Welcome to the Leaders Lab 1

Learning & Change

1. Learning to Lead 7
2. Career Planning for a Technology-Enabled World 12
3. Today's #1 Success Skill: Learning 16
4. You Can't See Yourself Completely: Asking for Feedback 19
5. How to Learn: Do It Your Way 23
6. Remain Grounded Amidst Massive Change 28
7. During Change, Handle Fear First 32
8. Leading Change: Address Different Types in Your Strategy 36

Strategic Productivity

9. The Day That Got Away 43
10. Make Room for the New 46
11. The Truth About Multitasking 49
12. Don't Spend More Than Ten Minutes on This 52
13. Information Overwhelm: The Culling Cure 56
14. Accelerate! 60
15. Do It Once 64
16. Seven Flavors of "No" 68
17. Tired of SMART Goals? 71
18. Grinding Your Gears? Take a Refresh Break 74

19. Feeling Stressed? Under Pressure? Seven "A"s to Ease Your Way	78
20. Seven Ways to Decide	81
21. Beyond SWOT: Five Simple Strategy Models	85
22. The Single Most-Effective Productivity Strategy	90

Creativity & Innovation

23. Help! I'm Not Creative!	95
24. Ignite Your Creative Capacity	99
25. When to Bother With Creativity	102
26. Creative Opportunity List	106
27. Should Brainstorming Be Banned?	109
28. Backward Bugs: Turn Complaints and Annoyances Into Solutions	113
29. Stuck? Change Your View	116
30. That's Funny! Humor as a Creativity Tool	119
31. Creative Destruction: Break It	122
32. Innovation: It's Not Just About New Products	125
33. Need Innovation Ideas? Listen to Your Customers	130
34. Not Feeling Creative? Your Role in Innovation	133
35. Unveil Your New Idea Strategically	137

Communication, Collaboration & Influence

36. Full-Bodied Listening	143
37. Ask, Ask, Ask: The Power of Questions	146
38. Showing Up as Your Best: The Impact of Nonverbal Communication	151

39. May I Have Your Attention, Please?	155
40. Make Your Message Memorable	158
41. Prepare Your Audience	161
42. In a World of Too-Much-Information, Less Is More	165
43. Watch Your Language!	168
44. Got Stage Fright?	172
45. How to Get People to Speak Up in Meetings	176
46. Eight Ways to Accomplish More in Less Meeting Time	180
47. Can We Just Talk?: When to Stop Arguing and Dialogue Instead	184
48. Moving Ideas Ahead: The BRAIN Process	188
49. Your Influence Map: Who You Need to Know to Get Things Done	191
50. How to Increase Your Influence Without Becoming CEO	195
51. How to Influence Someone	197

Developing Teams & Talent

52. Your Strengths Strategy	205
53. Beyond Potential: How to Develop Your Talents	209
54. What About Weaknesses?	214
55. The "Feeling Factor"	217
56. Seven Ways for Women to Come Across More Powerfully at Work	222
57. Be a Talent Magnet	229
58. Hiring Accountable People	232
59. Collaborative Teams: How to Make 2+2=5	237
60. Without This, You Won't Get Much Done	241

61. Don't Clog the Pipeline: Streamline Decisions   246

62. Where to Set Your Challenge Thermostat   249

63. Tailored Delegation   253

64. Are You Dreading Performance Reviews?   257

65. Update Your Motivation Methods   262

66. Put Humor to Work   267

Appendix

Notes   275

Bibliography   282

About the Author   287

Introduction: Welcome To The Leaders Lab

Lab: a space for experiments, research, teaching, and learning

Come on in.
Begin anywhere.
Research, experiment, discover.
Hone your leadership skills, strategies, and style.
Accelerate your leadership learning and progress.
Share, collaborate, and grow.
Lead yourself. Lead others. Lead thinking. Lead action. Lead progress.

Who Leaders Lab Is For

This book is a resource for forward-thinkers, learners, innovators, and leaders of all kinds. Specific types of leaders who will particularly benefit from this book include:

- **High-Potential Professionals** desiring to learn quickly to be prepared to step into bigger roles.
- **Experienced Leaders** looking to update and upgrade their leadership skills to thrive in changing times.
- **Smart Specialists and Experts** aspiring to increase their influence and advance in organizations.
- **Women and Minority Managers** seeking ways to capitalize on their strengths to break through to the next level.
- **Team Leaders** aiming to attract and develop talent, optimize collaboration, and improve results.
- **Innovators and Entrepreneurs** hoping to leverage opportunity.
- **Reluctant Leaders** wanting to boost their confidence and capability when they need to lead.

What You'll Learn
Among other things, *Leaders Lab* will help you:
- Get noticed (in a good way).
- Anticipate and successfully navigate change.
- Increase your influence, even if you don't have a big, fancy title.
- Boost your capacity to create and innovate.
- Communicate with impact to cut through the noise of the information era.
- Build, engage, and activate high-performing teams.
- Accomplish more and get the right things done.
- Expand your range of leadership strategies and tools.
- Hone your individual leadership style.
- Stay ahead of the career curve.

Leaders' Common Challenges
In more than ten years of coaching leaders of all kinds, I've found that while no two leaders, organizations, or situations are exactly alike, common problems and patterns tend to arise. If asked what they thought they needed or wanted to work on, clients would consistently list issues such as:
- "Selling myself and my ideas"
- "Dealing with office politics"
- "Motivating my staff"
- "Time management" and "Work/life balance"
- "Getting ahead"

As they advanced, "soft skills" became a significant factor in both performance and promotions.

In response, *Leaders Lab* covers a broad range of next-level thinking, communication, influence, productivity, team and talent development strategies to help you cultivate the mindset, qualities, and skills needed to succeed as a leader.

Skills and Strategies for This Era and Beyond
Certain challenges have intensified in today's rapidly changing, 24/7, information-rich world. For instance, modern communication tools make it possible to send messages instantly around the world, yet it's harder to command and hold your audience's attention. New technologies have disrupted many traditional careers and industries, while opening the way for new ones. Leaders must adapt, watch for opportunity, and develop increased capacity for learning, innovation, and change.

Anticipating both traditional leadership challenges and continued rapid change, *Leaders Lab* combines the best of timeless leadership thinking with breakthrough skills and strategies for the future.

Leaders Lab Approach: Accelerated, Individualized, Active Learning

This book is different from most leadership books in several ways.

Accelerated Learning: You're busier than ever. Acknowledging that your time is precious, *Leaders Lab* provides a comprehensive approach to leadership learning in manageable doses. You can zero in on just what you need and move as quickly as you like. Think of it as "bite-sized leadership learning."

Individualized Learning: Recognizing that today's leaders come in all sizes, shapes, roles, and varieties, *Leaders Lab* encourages you to develop your own authentic and effective style. Try out different strategies and approaches and then evaluate and adjust to find what works best for you and your situation.

Active Learning: Understanding leadership principles and thinking about leadership strategies is a good start, but they must be put into practice. *Leaders Lab* is designed to help you address current issues you face in practical ways.

You're invited to apply each strategy in your own context. Experiment. Practice. Evaluate. Adjust. Connect and combine new learning with what you already know.

To help you individualize and activate your learning, six elements are presented for each topic:

> **The Challenge:** A problem faced by many leaders
>
> **The Question:** A question phrased for solution-finding
>
> **Consider This:** Topical inspiration and thought-provoking quotes
>
> **Try This:** Strategies to explore
>
> **Apply & Evaluate:** Encouragement to experiment and assess your results. Tailor the strategy to your situation and style. Try it on to find your fit. Then consider three questions about the outcome and potential further applications.
>
> **Take Action: Now What?:** A summary for further action or link to a related topic

Think of me as your coach. We'll draw upon what you already know and expand your leadership capacity.

How to Use Leaders Lab

Recognizing your need for substance, flexibility, and speed, this book is designed to be used three ways. Choose the approach or combine the approaches that work best for you:

1) **Exploration**
   - **Start anywhere.** Check out topics that intrigue or stretch you.
   - **Chew on relevant, bite-sized pieces.** Pull *Leaders Lab* out and work with it regularly in small doses to help you address your current challenges.

2) **Comprehensive Leadership Learning**
   Use *Leaders Lab* as the foundation for an ongoing leadership learning program for yourself or your team. (See *Learning to Lead*, p. 7.)

3) **Resource for Ongoing Leadership Learning**
   Use *Leaders Lab* in conjunction with a coaching or team-building program; to supplement other leadership development materials and resources; in discussion forums, book clubs, or learning groups. Choose and work with the sections relevant to your program.

Leadership learning is an ongoing process. My hope is that you will turn to this book often along your way.

Be curious.
Experiment.
Make it your own.
Create a dialogue in your work- or play-place.
Learn. Grow. Thrive.

Welcome to the Leaders Lab. Come on in. Begin anywhere.

LEARNING & CHANGE

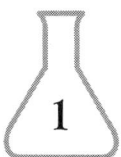 1   Learning To Lead

The Challenge: Learning to Lead
Sometimes we choose to lead. Sometimes we're placed in roles that ask us to—or demand that we do. Some aspects of leadership may come naturally to you. Some may not.

The Question: How Can You Become a Better Leader?
Leadership learning involves mindset, character, skills, strategies, and style.

Leadership Is Not "One-Size-Fits-All"
In coaching leaders of all kinds for more than ten years, I've found that no two leaders, organizations, or situations are exactly alike. What works for a 50-year-old male probably won't work well for or feel appropriate to a 25-year-old one. Women and minorities face particular challenges. What is appropriate in a formal corporate culture might seem ridiculous in an entrepreneurial one. The norm in one industry might be taboo in another. Complex problems may require collaboration with diverse specialists and stakeholders. There is often no one right answer.

Leadership Is Multidisciplinary
Successful leadership is rarely a matter of applying a single skill or a quick fix, but rather a synthesis of skills, strategy, and style. Advanced knowledge or a brilliant vision, for instance, might be lost without the concurrent ability to communicate, connect, and activate it.

Leadership Is Active
Leadership begins with thinking, but is expressed through action.

Consider This

"Leaders learn by leading, and they learn best by leading in the face of obstacles. As weather shapes mountains, problems shape leaders. Difficult bosses, lack of vision and virtue in the executive suite, circumstances beyond their control, and their own mistakes have been the leaders' basic curriculum."
—Warren Bennis

"In the tenuous years that lie ahead, the familiar benchmarks, guideposts, and milestones will change as rapidly and explosively as the times, but the one constant at the center of the vortex will be the leader. The leader beyond the millennium will not be the leader who has learned the lessons of how to do it, with ledgers of "hows" balanced with "its" that dissolve in the crashing changes ahead. The leader for today and the future will be focused on how to be—how to develop quality, character, mindset, values, principles, and courage."
—Frances Hesselbein

Leadership experts James Kouzes and Barry Posner conduct regular research on what followers expect from their leaders. The results consistently point to four key leadership characteristics. Most important, chosen by 85% of respondents is *"Honest,"* followed by *"Forward-Looking"* (70%), *"Inspiring"* (69%), and *"Competent"* (64%).[1]

Try This: Your Own Comprehensive Leadership Learning Program

Use this book as the foundation of your own leadership learning program by following this ten-step process:

1) **Adopt a Leadership Mindset**

   Leadership is not dependent on rank or position. On paper, we find formal leaders designated by official titles. In practice, though, leaders are found throughout communities and organizations at all levels and in all sorts of roles.

   True leaders are the ones who choose to initiate, create, influence, and inspire. They anticipate, envision, connect, model, build trust, empower, and guide to move people and ideas forward.

   Being a leader requires thinking beyond today and thinking beyond yourself. Being out in front often involves risk and discomfort. It requires commitment and, often, courage to be visible, pursue new ideas, take unpopular stands, and endure criticism. Effective leaders provide not only compelling words, but an inspiring example.

Do you choose to lead? Why? If you don't choose to lead, what are the likely consequences?

2) **Choose Your Leadership Role**
Wherever you are, there are opportunities to lead. You may have an official leadership title or you may take on the role of leader informally. You may be a leader in your current workplace or you may take on a leadership role in the community.

Lead yourself. Lead others. Lead thinking. Lead design. Lead activity. Lead value. Lead change. Lead progress.

You will learn best and grow fastest if you have a place to apply your learning immediately.

Where do you choose to lead?

3) **Lead Yourself First**
As a leader, others will look to you to provide an example. You need not be perfect to lead. In fact, showing that you are human may increase your likability. As a leader, you will be expected to model what you want from others, however. They'll look to you for commitment, competence, and consistency.

Before you step out to influence others, step back and check your motives. *Why do you aspire to lead? What do you hope to accomplish in the long run? How will your purpose benefit others?* If your mission is a selfish one, it's likely to be short-lived.

Consider the classic leadership question: *Why should I follow you?*

4) **Take Stock**
How will you lead? To be most effective, consider two factors—your unique leadership style and your organization's culture.

While you may appreciate and learn from watching other leaders, you must ultimately find your own way. Your special combination of strengths, qualities, values, and natural preferences influences what you pay attention to and how you get things done. Spend some time getting to know yourself. Assessments such as the StrengthsFinder® and Myers Briggs Type Indicator® can be useful in helping you understand your natural style and strengths, as well as how to bring out the best in others.

Know the culture in which you're working; that is, the norms—what behaviors are expected, what's rewarded, and how things really get done. Depending on your role, you probably have both the opportunity to create or affect the culture in your closest circles and the need to adapt to the culture of your larger organization or environment.

5) **Define Leadership Learning Goals**
Look ahead. *What kind of leader do you want to be? What do you need to learn? Which skills and qualities do you want to develop?* As you develop your goals, check out *Asking for Feedback* (p. 19), *Your Strengths Strategy* (p. 205), *Career Planning for a Technology-Enabled World* (p. 12), and *Tired of SMART Goals?* (p. 71).

6) **Devise a System**
Build a learning plan into your daily and weekly schedule. Devote regular attention to developing skills, learning strategies, and cultivating leadership qualities. For instance, you might take on one topic weekly.

There are many ways to learn; choose the ones that work best for you, whether that involves observing, experimenting, reading, attending classes, working with a coach, or participating in learning groups. (See *How to Learn: Do it Your Way*, p. 23.) Consider joining a learning group or connecting regularly with a learning partner, mentor, or coach who will help you stay focused.

7) **Practice for Mastery**
The most important part of the learning process is putting it into practice. Immediately apply your learning in your daily work. Then evaluate your results, adjust as needed, and practice until the new way of thinking or acting becomes natural. If you don't find opportunity to apply the learning in your current position, find outside projects or volunteer opportunities that provide hands-on experience.

8) **Extend the Value**
Keep looking for ways to use your learning and connect it with what you already know. As you master new strategies and skills, combine them to create powerful results. Model and share your learning with your team.

9) **Challenge Yourself**
Stretch your thinking and expand your leadership toolkit. Continually challenge yourself to move a little outside your comfort zone to meet new people, entertain new ideas, gain new experience, and increase your visibility.

10) Evolve as a Leader

The concept and practice of leadership is evolving as humans progress and innovations contribute to our increased reach, speed, opportunity, and potential. Today's communication and productivity tools present both new possibilities and new challenges for leaders.

The best leaders constantly upgrade and update their skills and strategies. Rather than latching onto each new fad, your aim should be to continuously progress by cultivating thinking, skills, and qualities to build your leadership capacities for the long haul.

Apply & Evaluate: What Do You Notice?

Start by reflecting on why, where, and how you want to lead. Determine your specific learning goals and system. Carry out your plan and apply what you've learned. Evaluate your progress, make needed adjustments, and continue your leadership evolution. As you do, also think through:

- *How will you stay focused on becoming a better leader?*
- *Who can provide additional useful feedback and suggestions? Who will support you in your learning?*
- *What can you do to encourage and support others in developing their leadership capacities?*

Take Action: Now What?

Observe effective leaders in a variety of fields—business leaders, political leaders, thought leaders, and innovators, for instance. Notice what they do that inspires others to listen, act, and follow. Notice how leaders can be successful using very different styles. Consider what will work best for you.

Leaders are needed at all levels and in all sorts of roles. Keep in mind that your power as a leader will expand as you help create other leaders.

# Career Planning For A Technology-Enabled World

The Challenge: Jobs of the Past Are Disappearing
It's hard to find any job or profession that has not been affected by the technological developments of our era. Some jobs are disappearing completely, while many others are being performed more efficiently using software, robots, or other technology-enabled methods.

Clearly, technological, economic, and demographic trends are upsetting our traditional ways of looking at work and careers, while providing whole new worlds of opportunity.

The Question: What's a Human to Do?
New jobs and entire new professions are emerging that involve new technologies—jobs in development, programming, applications, and management. While sci-fi movies may foretell a different scenario, for now someone will have to "tell the computer" what to do.

As new technological applications continue to alter processes, policy, and profitability in every field, even nontechnical careers are requiring basic technological competence and more frequent upgrading and updating of skills.

As time and technology march on, there will be no turning back—only moving forward to learn new skills and take on different types of roles. For the well-prepared and ambitious, current trends combine to provide more information, more opportunities, and more choices. Thinking ahead, you may be wondering:
- *What "good jobs" will be available in the future?*
- *What skills will be needed and valued?*
- *Where should I invest my learning time and energy?*

> **Consider This**
>
> *"The factory of the future will have only two employees, a man and a dog. The man will be there to feed the dog. The dog will be there to keep the man from touching the equipment."*
> —Warren Bennis
>
> *"The most exciting breakthrough of the twenty-first century will occur not because of technology, but because of an expanding concept of what it means to be human."*
> —John Naisbitt

Try This: Do What a Computer Can't Do

To thrive as the work world changes, be alert to trends that will create opportunities, make friends with technology, and increase your value by cultivating uniquely human skills.

Congratulations. You Got a Promotion.

The nature of human work is changing. On a higher level, this is good news. Most Americans are no longer "tilling the soil." In 1900, 40% of U.S. laborers were agricultural workers; by 2000, fewer than 1% were.[1] While there are still plenty of workers with aching body parts at the end of the day, our work generally is a lot less physical than in previous eras.

In this century, the shift continues. Much work that can be accomplished through routine movements and processes no longer requires human execution. Robots and machines can perform many manufacturing functions. Computers can crunch numbers. Software such as Turbotax can address standard scenarios. Google and Siri can access facts and perform routine administrative tasks.

Routine Jobs Are at Risk

In essence, "the computer," i.e. a technology-enabled system, does the "easy" stuff—the standard, routine functions.

Beyond Routine and Information-Gathering

You are left with the "tough stuff"—making judgments, creating systems, and handling exceptions. In a world overflowing with information, you are left to "cull"—that is, to decide what's important—and to "curate"—to put it together in meaningful forms. Such tasks require critical and constructive thinking.

Once More, With Feeling

You are also left with "the good stuff," the elements of work that touch others in uniquely human ways. Interpersonal skills—always a key factor in career advancement and success—have become more essential than ever. We are overloaded with data, but data doesn't move people. Those who can inspire and persuade through stories, humor, images, and other communication that cuts through the informational hubbub will garner distinct influence.

Connecting Dots and People

We are now operating in a larger, more complex world. With so many developments in science, technology, and other specialized fields, it has become difficult for any one person to know everything needed to solve complex problems. Collaboration is an increasingly vital skill.

The need to connect domains and ideas also requires social capital to connect and influence people, increasing the importance of being able to find, develop, and mobilize talent.

Now for Something Completely Different

Continued success will also depend on our ability to adapt and to create new forms of value. Be ready for this by updating your learning skills. Upgrade your proficiency in navigating change. Develop your capacity for creativity and innovation.

Lastly, because standing still is not likely to be a successful strategy for most workers, continue to increase your personal productivity and be ready to actively manage your career.

Skills for a New Era: "The New 7 Cs"

Putting the pieces together, then, along with basic technological competence, here are seven human skills needed to thrive in this era:

- **Changing:** Adapting effectively to new situations
- **Creating:** Generating new forms of value
- **Collaborating:** Connecting domains, ideas, and people effectively
- **Culling and Critical Thinking:** Pinpointing significant information and making good decisions
- **Communicating:** Using ideas and information to create meaning and inspire action
- **Coaching:** Developing and engaging talent
- **Career Skills:** Self-awareness, learning, personal productivity, and career management

Apply & Evaluate: What Do You Notice?
Take stock of your career skill sets and abilities. Imagine:
- *What types of work are we likely to insist be done by people, even if it becomes possible for them to be done by "computers"?*
- *Which of your skills are likely to continue to be valuable in the future? What new skills can you develop to thrive in this era?*
- *How can you learn and develop higher-level, uniquely human skills?*

Take Action: Now What?
Get started with a personal learning plan to prepare for the jobs of the future.

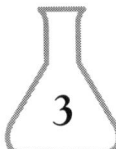 # 3 Today's #1 Success Skill: Learning

The Challenge: Having the Job Skills Needed in a Rapidly-Changing World

Entire careers have come and gone in the past few decades, as industries such as manufacturing, publishing, travel, entertainment, and more have been turned upside down by new technologies. By 2000, the National Research Council was already predicting that 50% of job skills would be out of date within 3-5 years.[1]

The speed of change continues to accelerate. Consider, for instance, that it took 46 years for electricity to be adopted by 25% of U.S. households (a benchmark indicating the start of mainstream acceptance and a springboard to related innovations), while the internet reached that benchmark within 7 years.[2] Innovations and technology applications can now spread even more quickly as word travels faster than ever.

Researchers from Oxford University predict that almost half of U.S. jobs could be automated by 2024.[3]

The Question: How Can You Prepare for the Jobs of the Future?

The question is not IF things will change, but how they will change. Consider:
- *What will the work world look like in the future?*
- *Where will the opportunity be?*
- *What will you need to learn?*
- *How can you learn most efficiently?*

Consider This

"Soon, just about every physical task you can imagine will be subject to automation. ... Machines will get the job done more quickly, accurately, and at a lower cost than you possibly can."
—Jerry Kaplan, *Humans Need Not Apply* (2015)

> *"The illiterate of the twenty-first century will not be those who cannot read and write, but those who cannot learn, unlearn, and relearn."*
> —Alvin Toffler

Try This: Take Charge With a Personal Learning Plan

It's impossible to determine exactly what the future work world will look like, but clearly technology, industries, and markets will continue to evolve and we will need to adapt. We will need to learn new ways of thinking and working.

Take Charge of Your Future

With such rapid change, it is likely that we will switch jobs and careers more frequently in the future. Learning not only increases your productivity and earning potential, but makes you more marketable.

Leaving career learning to employers or others is a risky proposition. Take charge of your career future to gain more control and increase your options. Doing so will allow you to design a path based on your individual talents, needs, interests, and goals. No one else will care as much about what is important to you.

Watch the Trends.

Get in the habit of trend-watching. Choose a few sources, such as *The Wall Street Journal*, tech-savvy friends, forward-looking websites, and industry association resources, to help you keep up.

Be Ready to Adapt

Imagine how things might look in 3-5 years. Look for opportunities to gain experience with emerging technologies. Become savvy about how change works —the typical stages we go through during change, how different types respond, how new ideas are adopted—and get good at working through it. Anticipate other skills that will be needed and valued.

Learn to Learn

Update and upgrade your learning skills. In this Information Era, learning is about much more than knowledge, memorization, and right answers. New skills, behaviors, mindsets, and modes of thinking will be required.

Besides traditional "book learning" and classroom activity, learning will increasingly involve dynamic methods:
- Gaining new experiences
- Expanding perspectives
- Connecting ideas
- Thinking differently
- Practicing and applying new skills
- Experimenting and adjusting
- Accessing resources and networks
- Adapting to change

Plan to Learn
Take charge of your career future by developing your own Personal Learning Plan. Define your personal purpose for learning. Decide what you want to learn. Choose the learning methods that work best for you, whether that's reading, attending workshops, working with a mentor or coach, observing experts, participating in forums, experimenting, getting practical experience as a volunteer, or another preferred method. Gather learning resources and set up a timeline for yourself.

Commit to your plan; then move ahead to create your preferred future!

Apply & Evaluate: What Do You Notice?
As you become more alert to trends, ask yourself:
- *Which trends are most likely to affect your career future?*
- *What do you need to learn to keep up, adapt, shift careers, or access new opportunities?*
- *How can you specifically prepare?*

Take Action: Now What?
Plan to spend at least 25% of your time each year taking on new challenges and learning. Consider career moves not only for better pay and titles, but for learning opportunity.

As a leader, encourage others to prepare for future careers through your example, an organizational culture that encourages learning, and support and resources for learners.

4. You Can't See Yourself Completely: Asking For Feedback

The Challenge: You Want or Need to Improve
Sometimes you know just what to work on; other times, it's not so obvious. You may have been surprised by criticism, or perhaps you have an inkling of something you'd like to improve, but not a clear idea of how to go about it. In such cases, it may be helpful to ask others for feedback, because we can't see ourselves completely.

The Question: How Can You Get Useful Performance Improvement Feedback?
To gather useful feedback, first understand what feedback is, different types you might receive, how it can be most productive, whom to ask, how to ask, and what to do with it after you receive it.

Consider This
> *"We all need people who will give us feedback. That's how we improve."*
> —Bill Gates

Try This: Solicit Future-Focused Performance Feedback
Do you dread the idea of asking for feedback? Most of us don't relish the idea of being criticized. We brace ourselves and prepare for the worst.

How Feedback Helps
There can be many benefits to receiving feedback. First, consider that you might receive positive feedback that will increase your confidence!

Additionally, you might:
- Become aware of how you are perceived.
- Find a starting point for improvement.
- Hear specific ideas on how to improve.
- Learn more about the person who is providing the feedback and what's important to them.
- Solidify or improve a relationship.
- Discover what's in your blind spots—either potential problems or positives you may not be able to see yourself.

It's Just Information
Some forms of feedback are fact-based and objective. You step on an accurate scale that reveals your weight, for instance. Feedback from people, though, is often subjective. As such, it may to some degree reflect personal opinions, experience, and biases. Even if it is not totally objective or accurate, it can be valuable as a sign of how you or your behaviors are being perceived.

If you dread the thought of receiving feedback that's not 100% positive, consider this: It's just information. Whether it's fact or perception, it may be useful to know. If you have the information, you can decide what to do with it.

Decide Which Type of Feedback You Want
A first step is often soliciting **general feedback** to zero in on key areas for development. Sometimes this general feedback is provided formally through surveys or "360 degree" reviews, which can also provide a starting point for gauging improvement. It might also be obtained informally by asking associates open-ended questions about their perceptions or even simply paying attention to reactions you are getting from others.

After reviewing this type of general feedback, the next step would be to ask for more **specific feedback** and suggestions. This part of the process, which focuses on ideas and actions for improvement, is usually the most useful part.

What Works
Feedback is most productive when:
- It focuses on the future.
- It focuses on 1–3 important areas.
- It includes specific suggestions on ways to improve.
- You are willing to listen, consider it, and, if appropriate, take action.
- It includes a way to follow-up to gauge progress.
- It is shared in a way both parties feel is safe.

Future-Focused Feedback Process

To obtain useful, future-focused feedback, take these five steps:

1) **Identify Productive Partners**

   If you have a choice of whom to ask for feedback, choose:
   - People you respect and trust.
   - People who know you and your work well enough to respond productively.
   - People in a variety of roles.
   - People who have a stake in your success.

   At work, consider including different types and levels of colleagues and contacts, such as superiors, subordinates, peers, customers, mentors, and coaches. Depending on your purpose, you may also want to ask people who see you outside of work, such as friends, family, and community members.

2) **Prepare**

   Be clear on your purpose for asking for feedback. Are you looking for an overall reaction and general areas for development OR are you looking for specific suggestions on an area you have already identified for improvement? Have you identified potential benefits of receiving feedback? Are you willing to listen, consider, and possibly act on feedback given?

   Do your homework. Know your starting point. For example, collect performance data, "360" results, or other information. Consider what's important to the person you are asking. Formulate questions that will elicit useful responses.

   Prepare the person you are asking in advance. Let them know what you are looking for. Ask if they are willing to help. If appropriate, mention how you plan to act on feedback and how giving you feedback may help them as well.

3) **Ask**

   After determining a starting point, solicit constructive future-focused feedback by asking questions such as:
   - *"How can I do better at ... in the future?"*
   - *"What suggestions do you have for me to improve at ... going forward?"*

If needed, ask a few more questions to clarify the response: *Tell me more about that. What would that look like? What would be an example?*

If appropriate, ask permission to follow up to see how you are doing.

4) **Listen**

When receiving feedback, be open and listen carefully. Thank the giver for their help and the information. Take in the feedback initially without judging it or defending yourself. You can evaluate it later and decide whether to act on it.

5) **Follow Up**

After you have carefully considered the feedback provided, you may want to ask for clarification and additional suggestions. Incorporate useful suggestions into your improvement plan.

If appropriate, follow up with your feedback provider at regular intervals by asking questions such as:
- *"How am I doing on ... since our last meeting?"*
- *"What other ways can I improve at ... ?"*

Don't Have Anyone to Ask?

Sometimes it's hard to find an appropriate person to ask for feedback. If you find yourself in that situation, explore other feedback methods. For instance, record yourself giving a presentation, play it back, and critique yourself; try different approaches and compare the results.

Apply & Evaluate: What Do You Notice?

Choose an area for improvement and solicit some feedback. Then assess the response:
- *What benefit did the information provide?*
- *What effect did your request have on your relationship with the person you asked?*
- *What's your next step?*

Take Action: Now What?

In some roles, we are set up to receive feedback automatically at regular intervals, such as with regular customer surveys or formal performance reviews. Consider supplementing that with your own methods of gathering feedback.

5. How To Learn: Do It Your Way

The Challenge: When it Comes to Learning, We're Not All the Same

Your sister loved school, but you hated it. I love to read, but you'd rather just plunge in and experiment. Sue gains a lot from listening to podcasts during her commute, but Sam understands the material better if he can see a chart or graph. Most of us grew up in schools that largely taught using one-size-fits-all methods, but in this era and, as adults, we usually have more choices.

The Question: What's the Best Way for You to Learn?

In this era of rapid change, "lifelong learning" is no longer just a trendy aspiration, but a firm requirement. Awareness of your learning preferences can help you identify the learning methods and options that will be most satisfying, efficient, and effective for you.

> **Consider This**
>
> *"You have your way. I have my way. As for the right way, the correct way, and the only way, it does not exist."*
> —Friedrich Nietzsche

Try This: Use Your Preferred Learning Methods

Start by exploring learning preferences from two standpoints: Modes and Styles.

Modes: What Kind of Learner Are You?

Do you learn best by seeing, hearing, or doing?

Whether you recognize it or not, you probably have a preferred mode of taking in and processing information. Learners generally prefer one of three modes of learning: Visual, Auditory, or Kinesthetic.

Visual Learners
Visual learners learn best by **seeing** a representation of material in pictures, demonstration, or writing. Diagrams, charts, maps, illustrations, video, and displays are effective learning tools for them. Reading and writing things down works well for those who also like to learn through written language. Visual learners might reveal their understanding through language such as "I can see ... ," "It appears ... ," or "I get the picture."

Auditory Learners
Auditory learners learn best by **hearing**. They learn well by listening and talking things through. Lectures, discussion, and recordings are effective learning methods for them. They might reveal their understanding through language such as "It sounds like ... ," "I hear you!" or "It clicked."

Kinesthetic Learners
Kinesthetic learners learn best by **doing**. Physical, tangible, practical activities, such as projects and experiments, work well for them. They tend to like hands-on activities where they can move around. They might use language such as "That feels right" or "I've got a grip on it." Have you known someone who wasn't very good at academics, but then was very successful in "the real world"? They might have been a kinesthetic learner.

Which mode do you prefer?
- ☐ Seeing
- ☐ Hearing
- ☐ Doing
- ☐ Combination

Learning Style
Along with these modal preferences, learners often have learning style preferences regarding format, structure, and type of content.

Format: Group vs. Individual Learning
Do you prefer to learn in a group or by yourself? While we are conditioned to learn in groups in school, some prefer to learn by themselves.

Group Learning

Learners who thrive in a group like to talk through ideas with and learn from others. They enjoy social opportunities and interaction. They are energized by group discussion and activities. Classes, workshops, team projects, discussion, and networking groups appeal to them.

In choosing group learning activities, group learners may also have a preference as to the type of group. Sometimes it helps to be surrounded by people who stretch you. They may provide inspiration as role-models, push you to reach for a higher level, and impart tough feedback. If you would benefit from a competitive environment, look for a group that will challenge you.

Other times and for certain types of learning and change, it works best to be in a group that provides encouragement and support in a safe environment. In these cases, it helps to be in a group of caring people with whom you can feel comfortable talking openly.

Individual Learning

Some learners prefer working on their own. Individual learning allows them to set their own direction and work at their own pace. They may appreciate privacy. They may perceive group work and rapport-building to be a waste of time and, thus, shy away from discussion groups and team projects. Reading, researching, journaling, taking an online course, or working one-on-one with a coach might appeal to them.

Which do you prefer?
- ☐ Group Learning
  - ☐ A group that will challenge me
  - ☐ A group that will support me
- ☐ Individual Learning
- ☐ Combination

Learning Structure: Formal vs. Informal

Learners may also prefer different amounts and types of structure.

Formal

Some learners work best with a formal, defined learning process. Clear structure and organization appeal to them. They look for a prepared syllabus, clear objectives, and a firm schedule. They like to know in advance exactly what to expect and what will be expected of them.

Informal
Others prefer a more free-flowing approach. They may appreciate having options to explore what is most interesting, relevant, or needed at the time. A structure that allows for spontaneity, flexibility, and individual choice appeals to them.

Which type of learning structure do you prefer?
- ☐ Formal
- ☐ Informal

Learning Content: Conceptual vs. Practical
Some learners are most interested in developing their thinking, while others are most interested in practical applications.

Conceptual Learning: Principles, Ideas, Meaning
Conceptual learners enjoy learning principles, identifying patterns, exploring meaning, and generating ideas. They value learning scenarios that allow them to understand concepts, connect and synthesize knowledge, develop strategies, and imagine possibilities.

Practical: Specific, Immediate Applications
Practical learners look for learning that can be immediately applied. They value tips, facts, examples, and specific useful information. Role plays, simulations, observation, projects, experiments, and other hands-on activities usually appeal to them.

Which type of content appeals more to you?
- ☐ Conceptual
- ☐ Practical
- ☐ Some of both
- ☐ It depends on the topic

"Sticky" Learning
For learning that sticks, include these three elements in your plan:
1) **Continuity:** Learning is a process, not a one-time event. Keep your learning in focus by reviewing it regularly. Claim it, practice it, and build on it.
2) **Active Learning:** For optimal results, combine multiple learning methods, including at least one active method. For instance, read and then apply your learning in a project; attend a class and then explain

what you learned to someone else; or learn principles and then use them in role-plays of potential real-world scenarios.

3) **Application:** Most importantly, apply your learning to something meaningful to you, whether that's in a breakthrough project at work or in important conversations at home.

Apply & Evaluate: What Do You Notice?

Think back to learning experiences that have worked well for you. Then determine:
- *Which learning formats work best for you?*
- *What learning options are available to you that incorporate your learning preferences?*
- *How will you make your learning "stick"?*

Take Action: Now What?

As you design your Personal Learning Plan, keep your preferred learning mode and style in mind. Choose options that fit with how you like to learn and learn most effectively.

Then move ahead with your plan, evaluating your progress at regular checkpoints along the way. Celebrate your achievement and keep moving forward with new learning goals.

 # Remain Grounded Amidst Massive Change

The Challenge: We Are Experiencing Massive Change
Technology and globalization are enabling change to occur with unprecedented speed and scope.

The Question: How Can You Remain Grounded While Everything Around You Is Changing?
Fortunately, not everything will change.

> **Consider This**
>
> *"We must accommodate changing times, but cling to unchanging principles."*
> —Former U.S. President Jimmy Carter
>
> *"It isn't the changes that do you in, it's the transitions."*
> —William Bridges

Try This: Be Change-Savvy
In the midst of change, we may not realize its extent or even recognize that it is transpiring at all. While it's relatively easy to embrace some types of progress, it can be disheartening to think that something good we've experienced in the past will change.

Understanding a few principles about change will help you be aware of how it occurs and how you can navigate it purposefully.

What DOESN'T Change
You can be sure that many things will change. Discoveries, innovations, demographic trends, economic conditions, politics, and other large-scale factors lead, in turn, to changes in markets, work, social attitudes, relationships, and

everyday life. Some of these changes are a permanent part of human "progress," while others, such as fashions, fads, and some economic conditions, are temporary or cyclical.

When it seems that everything is changing around us, we can usually count on certain factors to remain constant:

Who You Are: Your "core" is still the same. For instance, core personal values usually don't change significantly throughout one's lifetime, although the focus, emphasis, and means of expressing them may shift. If your personal value is "Family," for example, it may be manifest quite differently at different stages of your life. One who holds "Learning" as a core value may show up first as an enthusiastic student and avid reader and later as a proactive career skill builder. In this era, they might be taking multiple courses at their own convenience through a MOOC (Massive Open Online Course), such as Coursera. While the form, methods, or venues may change, the essence of the value endures.

Some Inborn Preferences: "Handedness" is one example of a preference we are born with that doesn't change. The vast majority of people naturally favor one hand over the other, although with effort they may be able to develop skill with either. We also have certain types of thinking preferences that usually remain the same, although we can and do expand on them to adapt to the demands of our circumstances. For instance, individuals usually have a preference for making decisions either using logic first or feelings first.

Universal Truths and Principles: Some truths are timeless. For instance, although expressed in slightly different ways, the principle of "The Golden Rule" has remained a foundational tenet of a diverse range of religions and societies throughout the ages. While technology and globalization are breaking down some barriers of time and space, we are still subject to the force of gravity.

Stages of Change

Change experts generally agree that we go through three stages during the change process.

During the **"Letting Go"** stage, we recognize an ending of the old and the need to change. In this stage, we may need to accept some discomfort, seek out information, and get support. Some find it useful to acknowledge the ending with some type of observance or "closure" process, such as a memorial service, graduation ceremony, handover, or major cleaning event.

The **"Transition"** stage can be the trickiest part, because it usually entails a degree of ambiguity and uncertainty. It can be a time of learning, opportunity, choice, and struggle as you create your future. It may be difficult to break old patterns, but also energizing to explore alternatives as you start moving toward something new. During this stage, be patient with yourself and others as you work things out. Take care of your mental, spiritual, emotional, and physical health. It can be helpful to find someone you can trust to talk with during this period.

Then, in the **"Let Come"** stage, you move forward with a new beginning. Keep your desired outcome in mind; also be willing to be surprised by new possibilities that emerge. Build momentum by celebrating small successes. Be alert to adjustments that are needed as things play out. Recommit to your vision and look ahead to what's next.

Navigating Change
Apply these three strategies to prosper as you navigate change in your work and life:

1) **Know, but don't limit, yourself.** Be confident in your core. Your highest values will keep you grounded during crisis and change. Be open to greater possibilities for yourself, though, as discoveries and innovations open the way for new ways to express your values, develop your capacities, and increase your impact. Reevaluate limitations under new light.

2) **Anticipate change.** Way back around 500 BC, Greek philosopher Heraclitus counseled, "There is nothing permanent except change." Even today, his observation holds. In the midst of today's widespread changes, it may seem hard to envision anything more, but further change is inevitable. If you can anticipate even a small part of it, you may be able to use that to your benefit and for the benefit of others.

3) **Focus on what you can control.** The world may be changing around you, but you can choose what you embrace and how you respond. Consider what you are in control of during change. Prepare. Think constructively. Take action. Learn. Even when you're not totally in control, you may have more influence than you first think. Investigate the implications. Explore opportunities. Create options. Build relationships. Shape perceptions. Refine your thinking. Upgrade your beliefs. Adopt a productive mindset. Improve your skills. Adjust your habits.

Apply & Evaluate: What Do You Notice?
Consider the role of change in your work and life:
- *What changes can you anticipate?*
- *What will not change?*
- *How can you prepare, think, and act for the best outcome during change?*

Take Action: Now What?
Adaptability is a key to success in this era. Consider ways to increase yours. Opportunities to thrive have never been greater for those who can anticipate and act on change.

7 During Change, Handle Fear First

The Challenge: Logic Is Not Enough to Move Most People to Change

Leaders often assume that facts, logic, and decrees will move people to change. In practice, exhaustive analysis, brilliantly-designed strategy, and authority will only take you so far. Strategies and processes are carried out not by themselves, but by people. For change to be fully successful, people must embrace it wholeheartedly.

The Question: How Can You Get People to Embrace Change?

If your change involves humans, pay attention to people and feelings, as well as to strategy and logic.

> **Consider This:**
>
> *"Frightened people never learn."*
> —John le Carré, *The Secret Pilgrim*
>
> *"People change what they do less because they are given analysis that shifts their thinking than because they are shown a truth that influences their behavior."*
> —John Kotter

Try This: Human-Centered Change

Keep the human aspects of change in mind as you plan and carry out your change strategy.

Handle Fear First

People are often fearful during times of change. What appears as resistance is really fear of failure, fear of loss, or simply fear of the unknown. Underlying these fears, they may be worrying: *I can't do it. It looks bad for me. I'm not in control.*

A change leader can either stoke the fear or transform it into positive energy. Sheer fear can be very effective to get people moving, but often brings about unproductive side effects as they take cover and focus on protecting themselves. When people are too fearful, they're unlikely to be at their best. There are several steps a change leader can take to reduce fear so that it is easier for others to embrace change and dedicate their best efforts toward making it work.

While you may not be able to remove the uncertainty underlying fear, you can address it by: 1) inspiring confidence, 2) showing compassion, 3) communicating strategically, and 4) providing an element of control.

Confidence: We Can Handle Whatever Comes Along

The key to confidence is knowing that you can handle whatever comes along. To inspire confidence, show evidence of one or more of these:
- *We've done it (or something similar or harder) before. We can do it again.*
- *Others have done it before.*
- *If our plan doesn't work at once, we'll figure it out.*

Compassion: We're Dealing With People Here

Consider the impact of change on people. Acknowledge feelings. Address fears. Fairness, respect, and empathy will go a long way for all concerned.

Communication: You're In on Things

Stimulate motivation, build trust, and manage expectations through strategic communication:

Paint a Positive Outcome

The way is easier when the goal is desirable. Paint a picture of the positive outcome you are envisioning. Be sure it's one that is achievable. If your goal is difficult or likely to take a long time to achieve, consider aiming for a shorter-term destination first.

Faced with change, people naturally ask themselves, "How will this affect me?" Change often involves initial discomfort or loss, so show as much benefit as possible. Make the benefits visual and tangible. Address what is important to individuals.

Personal Consequences

This is not to suggest sugarcoating the need for change. Even when the need is obvious and the change is positive, some impetus may be required to overcome inertia and get things moving. Change requires energy; it is usually just simpler to follow the status quo. People need to understand—and internalize—why change is needed and why it's important for them to act at once.

You may need to show what will happen if nothing changes. Demonstrate the potential consequences. Logic may be enough to convince some, but most will need to *feel* the necessity for change themselves.

"Oh, I Get It!"

An example of this is the smoker who tried for years to quit because his doctor had repeatedly warned him of the health risks. One day he witnessed his young son imitating him smoking. In a moment, it clicked. The consequences of continuing to smoke became clear in a dramatic, personal way; he realized that his habit affected his child's future, as well as his own. The smoker's love for his son emerged as his paramount motivation and he quit "cold turkey."

Consider what is most important to others. Aim for the "Oh, I get it!" response.

Manage Expectations

Most change efforts are not completely successful right away. Things often get worse before they get better. New behaviors require practice. In real life, processes don't always work as predicted. Adjustments are often necessary as unintended consequences surface.

Let people know you are committed to the outcome you envision and prepared to work through obstacles to get there.

Overcommunicate

People crave information during times of change. If they don't get it, they may make up inaccurate or unproductive stories. Don't underestimate the need to consistently repeat your message. Reach people with their preferred communication methods. Be accessible. Show what you want by putting your words into action.

Make sure your message is getting through. Ask others to play it back to you. Gauge your results; then adjust your message or methods as needed.

Control: You Have Some Say

People will be less fearful and more committed to the change plan if they feel they have some control over their future. Before rolling out your change initiative in a big way, gather support from others whose help you'll need:

- **Criteria, Input, Choices:** Involve those who will have a stake in making the change work—decision makers, "influencers," gatekeepers, implementers and others. To the extent possible, share your decision-making criteria, allow an opportunity for input, and provide choices. Ask questions such as "From your perspective, what's most important here?" and "How can we make this work?"
- **Resources:** Be sure those involved have the resources to make the change successful, such as information, equipment, workspace, communication tools, budgets, and training. Align the organizational structure and reward system to support your desired change.

Acknowledge Progress, Evaluate, and Adjust

Set yourself up for early success. Even small wins will build momentum. Reward and publicize improvement. You will get more of what you pay attention to and reward.

As you move ahead, evaluate how your change process is working. Give your well-thought-out plans a chance to work. Then, if you are not seeing success, be willing to make adjustments. *What else could you try to get to the outcome you want? If it's not working, would smaller steps work better? Or is a more dramatic approach required?*

Apply & Evaluate: What Do You Notice?

As you develop and implement your change plan, consider:
- *What fears need to be addressed?*
- *How might you get stakeholders involved in the process early on?*
- *How can you support and encourage people during the process?*

Take Action: Now What?

As you plan, keep in mind that individuals will respond differently to change, depending on their interests, experience, and mindset. Be ready to adapt your approach to reach different types.

8. Leading Change: Address Different Types In Your Strategy

The Challenge: Individuals Respond Differently to Change
Because no two individuals are exactly the same, when you lead a change, your followers won't all perceive it and respond the same way.

The Question: How Can You Lead Change to Get the Best Results From the Greatest Number?

> **Consider This:**
> *"Normal people ... believe that if it ain't broke, don't fix it. Engineers believe if it ain't broke, it doesn't have enough features yet."*
> —Scott Adams

Try This: Address Different Types of Changers in Your Change Strategy

Horses and Water Analogy
It's said that "you can lead a horse to water, but you can't make it drink." Let's apply that analogy to leading change:
- Some of your horses won't need encouragement; they'll seek out water even before they're thirsty. (Ironically, many of them will be criticized for this by less forward-thinking horses. Why would they waste their time? And why waste time possibly looking in the wrong direction? After all, isn't it somebody else's job to provide water?)
- Some will seek out water themselves because they are thirsty.

- Some will drink the water if they come across it. They particularly like water. They know they'll want or need some soon. The water is cool, clear, attractive.
- Others will drink the water if you lead them to it. They need to know how to get there. They'll then realize, "Gee, I was getting thirsty," or "Hey, this is pretty good."
- Some, led to the water, will still need to be encouraged. "Hey, try this. How 'bout just one sip?"
- Some, led to the water, will still avoid it. You can try to push or pull their heads down into it. You can try to pry their mouths open.
- Some, even then, will refuse it.
- A few can't even be led over to the water. Perhaps they have a temporary condition that prevents them from "walking." You have to bring the water to them.
- Lastly, some can't be led because they've dug their heels in and won't budge. Eventually, if they become thirsty enough, they might partake. Or they may die.

Note: No "Kool-Aid" here. Just cool, clear water.

It's Personal: Situational Motivation and Fear

Depending on the nature of your change, individuals will respond differently according to their natural motivation and personal fears. You may be facing a collection of these different types of responders:

Welcomers

People are more likely to "drink the water" willingly, or even enthusiastically, if:
- The change is their idea.
- They can see significant benefits of the change.
- They had some input on the parts that will affect them.

To the extent that people feel they have some influence or control over their future, change will be more welcome.

Resisters

Some may resist, particularly if they:
- Sense personal risk, such as potential job loss or embarrassment.
- Fear losing large status quo benefits.
- Are skeptical, fearing the proposed change is just a first step and wondering when "the other shoe will drop."

Hesitaters
In between, others may hesitate if:
- Benefits are not clear.
- They like the orderliness of being "settled."
- They can see both potential benefits and pitfalls. Some of the smartest people will fear the most, because they can see more potential risks along with opportunities.

Be ready to address the Resisters' and Hesitaters' fears, while dramatizing benefits.

Different Breeds: Get the Best From Different Change Types
People will also react differently depending on their natural change proclivities. As you understand their different inclinations, you can specifically call upon each type during the parts of change that will allow them to shine and support them in the other stages.

Pioneers: Pioneers welcome change. They like to challenge the status quo, imagine a better future, and generate new ideas. They are usually enthusiastic changers, but not always practical finishers. Rely on them for concepts, vision, imagination, and enthusiasm. Fuel their contribution by encouraging their initiative and providing resources and support for exploration, smart risk taking, and innovation.

Builders: While Builders may not be the first to imagine or initiate change, when presented with a change idea, they figure out how to make it work. They develop systems and processes, acquire resources, and negotiate with other players to put the implementation pieces together. Present them with a vision and involve them in translating it into workable form.

Refiners: Refiners want things to run in an orderly way. As such, they may appear to resist change. If you can keep them from shutting down worthwhile ideas before they can be developed, their discipline and expertise can be very valuable at different points in the change process. Rely on them to anticipate problems, contribute expertise, evaluate, troubleshoot, and fine-tune.

Strategies to Address All Change Types
Recognizing that individuals will respond to a call for change differently, based on their type, interests, and experiences, include a range of strategies in your plan.

To obtain commitment to change:
- Provide opportunities along the way for input or involvement in planning it.
- Demonstrate the potential benefits in ways individuals can grasp, whether that's through some sort of tangible proof, testimonials from others like them who have made a similar change, or encouragement from respected opinion leaders.
- Model the behaviors you want to see from others.
- Reinforce the change you want to see by recognizing successes and aligning rewards.

To facilitate change implementation:
- Consider rolling out the change in stages.
- Make it simple to grasp and implement.
- Provide plenty of information and training.
- Provide an opportunity for feedback and adjustment.
- Be ready to adapt your approach for different types.

Apply & Evaluate: What Do You Notice?
As you design your change plan, take into account:
- *Who is likely to welcome change? Who might resist or hesitate?*
- *How can you get the strongest commitment from the greatest number?*
- *How can you involve different types (Pioneers, Builders, Refiners) in the parts of the change process they do best?*

Take Action: Now What?
As you carry out your change plan, look ahead to anticipate the inevitable subsequent changes that will occur.

STRATEGIC PRODUCTIVITY

9. The Day That Got Away

The Challenge: The Day That Got Away
Do you ever get to the end of the day and wonder why it didn't go as planned? You hardly had a chance to breathe, yet you don't have much to show for it.

The Question: Where Does the Time Go???
That's the question many of us ask, but rarely answer specifically and accurately. Knowing exactly where your time and energy are going is the first step in seriously improving your productivity.

Consider This

> *"Time is really the only capital that any human being has, and the only thing he can't afford to lose."*
> –Thomas Edison

Try This: Keep a Log This Week
Starting right now, keep track of your activity for a week. Unless you are in the midst of a highly unusual week, such as a Tahitian vacation or a once-a-year Boot Camp, don't wait for a perfect, or even "normal," day to begin; they rarely occur. Don't worry about how it will look. The idea is neither to show perfection nor to engender guilt, but rather to get a sense of reality. If seven days seems daunting, start with three days.

Keep a log. Write down each activity and the time you spend on it. For instance, if you attend a meeting, work on a project, take a break, answer a few emails, or make a phone call, jot it down along with the time. Note each time you switch activities. If you take on a lot of little activities, keep track in regular intervals, say every 15 or 30 minutes.

For instance:
> 9:00 a.m.: Staff Meeting
> 9:35: Coffee, emails
> 10:00: Client phone call/research
> 10:40: Sales proposal draft
> 11:15: Checked email, misc admin
> 11:40: Conversation with boss about x

Keep your log handy so you can track your activity in real time. Some find it easiest to keep their log in a spiral-bound notebook. Others keep it on their phone.

This will be just for your own use. If you think it's useful, you can show your log to someone else or talk over your findings later, but it's most important to do this for yourself. It's only useful insofar as it is honest and accurate.

Don't judge yourself as you do this or change your normal approach. Just record your activity as accurately as you can. At the end of the day, note your major accomplishments.

Keep track of your life outside of work, too. There's likely to be some overlap. You may discover recurring patterns and ways to make your whole life better.

If you get off track, start back up as soon as possible. You will, of course, be busy all week living and working, so you may not be able to or remember to write everything down. If that happens, record your best guess for how you used your time as soon as you can and then resume regular tracking.

If you find yourself resisting this, ask yourself why. What are you concerned about? This exercise is just for you. It will help you recognize activity patterns and provide a starting-point for improvement. Even a few small adjustments could make a noticeable difference in your stress level and output.

Keep going. Think of this exercise as a small investment toward potential big productivity gains. Make it as easy on yourself as possible. Don't suffer over it or overthink it. Just do it. You can decide later exactly how you want to use it.

Apply & Evaluate: What Do You Notice?

Review your log at the end of the week. Try to look at it objectively. Don't thrash yourself. Don't make excuses. Just note what happened.

What do you observe about how you used your time? Notice:
- Regular patterns
- Regular interruptions
- Surprises
- What you accomplished
- When and how you accomplish the most
- What you wanted to accomplish but didn't
- What keeps you from being most productive
- Who else is putting demands on your time
- What creates energy versus what zaps your energy
- How long things took versus how long you thought they would take

Take Action: Now What?

What do you see that you could adjust to immediately improve your productivity?

For instance, could you ...
- Avoid distractions?
- Anticipate demands and requests from others?
- Plan better?
- Figure out a way to say "no" graciously or negotiate more realistic deadlines?
- Adjust your schedule to give yourself a block of concentrated time to focus on your most important project?
- Get organized so you can find information you need often more easily?

Improvement is a process. Little tweaks can add up to make a big difference. Start with a couple of small adjustments, note your results, and continue to look for ways to boost your productivity.

10. Make Room For The New

The Challenge: Overflowing "To Do" Lists
The problem I most frequently hear from clients and other friends is their inability to find enough time to get everything done. Most have increasing demands at work and also long for better work-life balance. They know they need to take on new challenges and activities to progress, yet most feel stretched to keep up with their current demands.

If those predicaments are true for you, try this simple experiment. Fill a drinking glass with water. Then try adding more. Yes, you can probably "top it off" with a little more, but you will have to carry it very carefully or it will spill. Eventually there's no more room to fill the glass unless you empty some of the "old" water first.

This is the scenario many of us face when we want to take on more. We try to squeeze it in on top of our already-full load. One possible solution is to find ways to be more efficient with the old tasks. Another strategy might be to acquire better skills or resources. At some point, though, some of the old thinking, strategies, and activities must go to make room for new, more effective and productive ones.

The Question: What Can You Remove to Make Room?
Before you take on new goals and activities, consider these questions first:
- *Which old goals or strategies are no longer relevant?*
- *Which goals or activities on your list are really not very important to you?*
- *Which activities or strategies don't make a difference?*
- *Which old habits no longer serve you well?*
- *What do you no longer use or need that's taking up physical or mental space?*

> **Consider This**
>
> *"If you want to do something new, you have to stop doing something old."*
> —Peter Drucker

Try This: Make Room for the New

Make more room in your "glass" for the new with these strategies:

Whittle down your goals. Include just a few very clear and important ones. Write them down and keep them visible. Then design your daily activities around moving forward to accomplish these priorities.

Don't do what doesn't matter. Are there goals or activities you have taken on solely because others have suggested them or you feel you "should" do them? Consider how committed you are to each of your goals and activities; consider the possibility of dropping the ones that aren't really that important to you or your success.

Give yourself permission. Don't do things that don't make a difference. My homemade piecrust wasn't really any better than the kind available in the dairy case.

Examine your assumptions. Activities you once thought were important may no longer be. For example, a new boss may have different needs and priorities than the last. Customers may be using your products or valuing your services differently than in the past.

Update your habits. Examine your routines to see if they are currently serving you well. Sometimes we carry on with activities that worked well at a certain time (for instance, when we were single; or before we became managers; or before we used laptops and smartphones.) They may not all still be necessary or effective. Consider new ways to streamline routine activities by using new technologies. For example, you might set up automatic bill-paying, schedule virtual meetings, shop online, and use productivity apps.

Shift responsibilities. Consider the possibility of letting someone else take on activities you don't enjoy or don't do well. They might do it better, faster, or cheaper—and be glad to do it! Could you ask for or hire help, negotiate a change in responsibilities, or trade services?

Make room physically. Clean out and organize your space. Clear away distracting clutter so you can focus and find things more easily. Dump outdated equipment and documents. Remove items that aren't beautiful, useful, or loved.

Make room mentally. Honor what you've achieved during the last year. Acknowledge what you've learned. Release unproductive thinking. And then keep moving onward and upward.

Apply & Evaluate: What Do You Notice?
Notice how it feels to have fewer goals and activities on your list. Then consider:
- *What else could you stop doing or simplify?*
- *What other habits and assumptions could be updated?*
- *How often would it make sense for you to reevaluate and cull your lists?*

Take Action: Now What?
Before you add new goals or activities, increase your chances of accomplishing them by making room in your thinking, your schedule, and your space.

11 The Truth About Multitasking

The Challenge: More Things to Do Than the Time Available to Do Them

It seems we're all facing the more-things-to-do-than-the-time-available-to-do-them challenge these days. "Timesaving" technology has increased expectations of what we can accomplish and how quickly we can accomplish it. The boundaries between work, home, and anywhere else have become blurred. The younger generation routinely juggles several communication devices at once and their elders are catching on.

The Question: You Can Get More Done by Doing Two (or More) Things at Once, Right?

Probably not.

Multitasking Actually Decreases Productivity

We multitask to get more done, however, in general, taking on more than one task at a time actually decreases productivity. Productivity researchers have found that switching from task to task can cost you as much as 50% efficiency.[1] Shifting attention back and forth between different types of activities requires extra time to refocus.[2] Additionally, when our attention is divided, we are more prone to making mistakes. A productivity study conducted by Microsoft revealed that, after being interrupted by electronic messages, it took workers 10–15 minutes to return to their main task.[3] A University of London study found that constant emailing and text-messaging reduced mental capability by an average of 10 IQ points, which would be similar to the effect of missing a whole night's sleep![4]

It Can Be Downright Dangerous!

Drivers who text. A parent who get distracted while his toddler is in the bathtub. Multitasking emailers who accidentally "reply all," broadcasting embarrassing or incriminating messages. In some situations, splitting attention even for short periods can have tragic effects.

Some May Be Better Than Others at It
Whether skill can be attributed to genetics, generation, or pure practice, it does seem that some are better at multitasking than others. Brain researchers note differences in male and female brains that imply greater communication and cooperation between the two hemispheres in female brains,[5] which may give women an advantage. While it's generally assumed that "Net Geners" are better at multitasking, this may not be true. Research by the Institute for the Future of the Mind at Oxford concludes that 18-21 year-olds aren't any better than 35-39 year-olds in maintaining their concentration when interrupted by a phone call or an instant message.[6]

> **Consider This**
>
> *"To do two things at once is to do neither."*
> —Publilius Syrus

Try This: Focus and Finish
High-impact activities, such as thinking, planning, creating, deciding, prioritizing, and listening deeply, require mental focus and energy. Give yourself undistracted time and space to concentrate on these. Turn off your phone, email notifications, and other noise.

The bottom line: *"If you're trying to accomplish many things at the same time, you'll get more done by focusing on one task at a time, not by switching constantly from one task to another."*—Joshua S. Rubinstein, David E. Meyer, and Jeffrey E. Evans[7]

When Tempted, Consider Other Strategies
When you need to improve your efficiency, consider other productivity strategies before resorting to multitasking. Batch short tasks, such as reading and responding to routine email, instead of taking them on one at a time as they come. Look for tasks that could be delegated, automated, or simply ignored.

If You Must, Multitask "Autopilot" Tasks
Multitasking works best when one of the tasks doesn't require conscious attention and the other doesn't require much focus or mental energy. Watch a sitcom while doing repetitive physical tasks, such as simple sorting or routine exercises. Listen to music while you brush your teeth. Daydream while you

prepare a simple recipe you've been making for years, but not one you have to read. Text while you wait in line, but not while crossing the street. Parents, delete a few emails while you're on hold with the bank, but not while your teenager is trying to tell you something. And (*Net Gener eye-roll*) learn to use the features of your electronic devices so you, too, can navigate them on autopilot.

Apply & Evaluate: What Do You Notice?
Notice what happens when you try these tactics:
- Are you an average Smartphone user who checks your device 150 times a day? Turn yours off while you take on an important task that requires concentration.
- When someone you're trying to talk to is doing something else, notice how you feel and the effectiveness of the conversation. (Consider that next time you are the listener.) Pause until you have their attention.
- Figure out which tasks you can actually accomplish adequately as multitasks.

Take Action: Now What?
Recognize that you will usually come out ahead by concentrating on one thing at a time. Focus and finish. Listen completely. Act mindfully.

12. Don't Spend More Than Ten Minutes On This

The Challenge: Wasting Time On Things That Aren't Worth It
There are many reasons we may unnecessarily waste time on tasks—perfectionism, overthinking, failing to clarify what's really required before forging ahead, drifting, or approaching every task the same way.

The Question: What's Really Required Right Now?
Think about riding a ten-speed bike. Skilled bikers select specific gears to match the terrain. Selecting the most appropriate gear at any moment allows them to make the most of their energy traveling long distances at optimal speeds.

Similarly, we can operate in many different gears. We can improve our productivity by being alert to our choices and making optimal shifts. What does the terrain call for?

> **Consider This**
>
> *"Life is like a ten-speed bike. Most of us have gears that we never use."*
> —Charles Schultz

Try This: Shift Into the Optimal Gear
Determining standards up front for the work to be done can make a big difference in productivity. Being clear on the standards can save you from spending unnecessary time on one hand, or turning in unacceptable work on the other. Standards for any particular task might vary a great deal depending on the potential audience, the use for your work, and timing.

Standards: Quality, Detail, Accuracy

When assessing your priorities and planning for the best use of time, consider both the importance of the task and how well it needs to be done. Define these two factors for both your "to do" list and for tasks you delegate.

1) **How important is it?**
    - *What is the potential benefit?*
    - *What is the potential consequence or risk if it is not done?*
    - *How will it make a difference?*

2) **How well does it need to be done?**
    - *What is the level of quality, detail, or accuracy needed at this time?*

   Quality: How well does it need to be done? Depending on the task, the range might be:
    - *It doesn't matter at all how well it's done, just that an effort was made.*
    - *It doesn't matter much. It can be fixed later if necessary.*
    - *OK is good enough.*
    - *Good quality is important here.*
    - *Perfection will be appreciated.*

   Detail: How much detail is needed at this time?
    - *No detail, just broad strokes*
    - *Rough outline*
    - *Complete outline*
    - *Full detail*

   Accuracy: How accurate does it need to be for now? What's the tolerable margin of error?
    - *Rough guess (For example, within 20%, depending on the type of project)*
    - *Calculated guess (For example, within 5–10%)*
    - *Rough calculation (For example, within 1–5%)*
    - *Exact calculation*

Your prioritized to-do list might now look something like this:

<u>Task</u>　　　　　<u>Importance</u>　　　　　<u>Quality/Detail/Accuracy needed</u>

Timing: Shift Gears When the Terrain Calls for It

Note that your answers may vary depending on where you are in a process. For instance, early on in a project, you might find you need to be thinking mainly in "broad strokes." You need to test the waters and see if the idea is worth pursuing further. You certainly don't want to overlook potential risks, necessary details, and accurate information, but why spend too much time on that if you're going in the wrong direction? If you can get some fast feedback, you can adjust quickly without spending a lot of time on dead-ends. At certain points, say, before you commit large amounts of money or time, you'll want to double-check your assumptions, think through more detail, carefully consider possible risks, and make more exact calculations.

Consequences

Just as you would choose different speeds when traveling on a freeway versus traveling through a school zone, the work speed you choose might depend on how fast others are moving, as well as the consequences of moving too quickly or slowly.

What's the risk of a poor decision? Can you recover easily or do it over? Will it pass quickly, or will you have to live with it for a long time?

What's Your Tendency?

Speed can be an important factor in productivity. Depending on the situation and our personal tendencies, we may need to consciously speed up or slow down.

Some situations call for perfection—brain surgery, classical music competitions, or calculation of your paycheck, for instance. If you tend toward perfectionism, though, you may be slowing yourself down unnecessarily in some situations and severely compromising your productivity. Sometimes you might have to tell yourself, "It doesn't have to be perfect. It just has to be done!"

On the other hand, some make mistakes or have to redo work because they move ahead too quickly without thinking carefully enough. If this is your tendency, you may need to slow down, delve deeper, and pay more attention to details, consequences, and practicality.

Be aware of your natural tendencies and be ready to adjust as needed.

Apply & Evaluate: What Do You Notice?

Examine your to-do list:
- *What are the detail, quality, and accuracy requirements for each item?*
- *What's your "default" gear?*
- *What other gears would give you better productivity? How can you learn to more skillfully shift gears when the "terrain" calls for it?*

Take Action: Now What?

Choose the optimal gear for the speed, quality, level of detail, and accuracy your activity calls for.

If you are a manager, specify these during delegation conversations. If a project is being delegated to you and it's not clear, ask for clarification on the expected timeframe and standards.

13 Information Overwhelm: The Culling Cure

The Challenge: We're Drowning in Information
Are you overwhelmed by data? Having trouble keeping up? Do you feel like you'll never catch up on your reading? Have you used up your smartphone's storage capacity with too many apps? Is your time being sucked away surfing the net and trolling social media sites?

Some of the information on our paths is important, productive, and accurate. Some is not. David Shenk, author of *Data Smog: Surviving the Information Glut,* calls it the "noxious muck and druck of the information age."[1]

The Question: What Information Is Worthy of Your Attention?
We need to update our skills and productivity strategies to adapt to this explosion of information. I call this skill "culling"—selecting our information intake strategically.

Consider This

"The fog of information can drive out knowledge."
—Daniel Boorstin

"All of the books in the world contain no more information than is broadcast as video in a single large American city in a single year. Not all bits have equal value."
—Carl Sagan

"True genius resides in the capacity for evaluation of uncertain, hazardous, and conflicting information."
—Winston Churchill

Try This: Culling

To make best use of your attention, time, and energy when faced with TMI, Too Much Information, try these strategies:

Make Deliberate Choices

Recognize that many, in fact most, of the sources vying for your attention have a commercial purpose, even if it doesn't at first appear that they're trying to sell you something. Sometimes we forget this, especially when the services and sources we use appear to be "free." They may be making money by "harvesting your eyeballs," surrounding attention-getting information, entertainment, or services with paid advertising. They may be tracking your information as you search and consume it so they can sell that information to advertisers who can then market to you directly. (Notice the ads that pop up as you surf the internet and you'll see what I mean.)

Be mindful of the information you take in. Don't drift or let yourself be distracted by provocative headlines.

Direct Your Attention With Purpose

Since your attention has limits, aim it strategically. As you use the internet or other information sources, keep your purpose in mind and adapt your usage accordingly. For instance, your range of informational purposes today might include:

- **Awareness:** Top-level exposure to a topic or organization
- **Research:** Searching for specific information you will act on later
- **Action:** Information you will act on now, such as buying or sharing
- **Retention:** Information you want to keep, store, or remember
- **Challenging Your Thinking:** Information that provides new ideas, perspectives, and learning
- **Sourcing:** Searching for information sources so you know where to find more information if you need it in the future
- **Entertainment**

To use your time and attention efficiently, have a specific goal in mind when you search. For instance, if your purpose is awareness, you can usually skim headlines quickly. The first sentence or paragraph contains the main idea 90% of the time. If you are sourcing or researching, you'll need a system to retrieve the information or find the source later.

Speed is not always the best strategy. In *The Shallows: What the Internet is Doing to Our Brains*, Nicholas Carr writes that "when we go online, we enter an environment that promotes cursory reading, hurried and distracted thinking, and superficial learning."[2] If you want to explore new concepts, understand complex ideas, or retain facts, slow down so you can process them.

What Difference Will It Make?
Direct most of your attention where it makes the biggest difference:
- High-impact issues and activities
- Priorities
- Focused topics
- "Need-to-know" information
- Issues of long-term importance
- Information you will act on

Limit the attention you give to other material, such as:
- Information you don't need now, but can easily find again if needed
- "Nice-to-know" information
- Distractions that provide little benefit
- Redundant sources
- Entertainment

Leave some room for serendipity, creativity, and surprises, but direct most of your attention where it's likely to have the most impact.

Be Savvy and Selective About Your Information Sources
Know what you are looking *for*, and know what you are looking *at*. On the internet, there are few gatekeepers or fact-checkers. For the most part, anyone can say anything.

Consider your sources carefully. Are they credible? What's their purpose? Does the information represent fact or opinion? Is the information accurate and clear? Can you find what you're looking for easily?

Simplify. Strategize. Systematize.
Information overload creeps up on us. Revisit your habits. Dump old information. Slim down your intake. Get off insignificant mailing lists. Before you join new ones, ask yourself what else you could be doing with your time and attention.

Set up a system to regularly clear out paper, email, reports, and other accumulating information. Only collect what you will use. Set up your systems so you will know where you can find information when you need it.

Draw Boundaries
Don't engage in obvious time-wasters. Set limits on the time you spend "surfing." Give yourself permission to ignore unimportant distractions. Question yourself if you feel you have to check your devices every few minutes.

Limit the amount of time you will spend on a search or the number of sites you will search. This will be easier if you have chosen your sources well. (*I'll check prices on four sites. I'll find three pieces of research to support my point. I'll ask two friends for their opinion.*)

Use Leverage
It's hard to know everything. Access OPK, Other People's Knowledge, to broaden yours efficiently. Connect with "knowledge partners" in your network to exchange information and ideas. Find aggregators, sources that collect and transmit a summary of articles, on subjects that interest you.

Switch It Up
With so many information sources to choose from, we often stick to the ones we already know and are comfortable with, limiting our exposure to different perspectives. Experiment with new sources occasionally to expand your thinking. Try something broad and something deep. Sample something unique. Seek out a source with a contrasting view.

Apply & Evaluate: What Do You Notice?
Review the sources you are using for information. Notice the quality, accuracy, and variety of information you are taking in. Try adjusting your intake speed for different information purposes. Then identify:
- Which information sources are "keepers"?
- Which could you live without or replace with better sources?
- How can you improve your information efficiency?

Take Action: Now What?
Review and cull your regular information sources periodically. Switch out duplicative or weak sources for unique or stronger sources. Search for and consume information purposefully, adapting your level of attention, speed, and methods to your needs. Draw boundaries wisely to prevent overload. Consider ways to tap into efficient information resources.

14. Accelerate!

The Challenge: At This Rate, You'll Never Get to Everything
While you're facing higher expectations and juggling a heavier workload, you're probably also missing opportunities.

The Question: How Can You Get Things Done Faster?
Something's got to give.

Consider This

> *"The world is changing very fast. Big will not beat small anymore. It will be the fast beating the slow."*
> —Rupert Murdoch

> *"Speed is useful only if you are running in the right direction."*
> —Joel A. Barker

Try This: Practice Strategic Acceleration
Accomplishing things faster entails more than rushing about. Strategy is required.

Don't Do
First, look for ways you could move faster by NOT doing things. Are you busy with tasks that are no longer necessary or produce little? For instance, could you:
- *Forgo a task entirely?* (Would anyone miss it? Would anyone notice?)
- *Skip a step?*
- *Streamline?*
- *Start over a simpler way?*

One successful entrepreneur I know was so overwhelmed by email (he had more than 60,000 emails in his inbox), he decided his best move was to declare "email bankruptcy." After identifying obvious important messages, he deleted everything more than 45 days old. This is a dramatic move most of us wouldn't dare, but this entrepreneur figured anything important would come back to him at some point.

An example of skipping a step has occurred on a large scale in some less-developed countries where there's been a huge surge in phone usage over the past couple of decades. With new cell technology, it was no longer necessary to incur the investment and trouble of laying landlines. While the most-developed world has been adding and transitioning to cellphones, in these less-developed countries, users simply skipped directly to cellphones.

Imitate

Perhaps you've heard of VisiCalc spreadsheet software, goto.com's pay-per-click advertising, and Chux disposable diapers. It's more likely, though, that you're familiar with Excel, Google Adwords, and Pampers. Those in the first group were pioneers in their category, while the second group adopted their ideas and became market leaders.

Being a pioneer can be an exciting adventure! One can move a lot faster, though, where the path is already at least somewhat paved. Being the trailblazer can give you a "first-mover advantage," but its value may be minimal if your work is easily replicated. More often, you'll be better off saving the energy you might have spent bushwhacking and spending it instead making improvements that will set you apart and let you leverage someone else's start-up learning.

"Most everything I've done, I've copied from someone else."

—Sam Walton

Get Advice

An experienced guide can save you an enormous amount of time and effort. It may be worth hiring a professional, such as a finance, legal, or design expert, to advise you in areas of specialized knowledge. A mentor who has already been through a similar journey can help you navigate political issues and find resources. A coach can help you develop your talents and activate your potential. Honest feedback and advice from a skilled partner can help you avoid the bogs and direct your energies most productively.

Leverage Systems

What a relief that we don't have to always create everything from scratch or handle every detail! Look for existing platforms, systems, and networks that provide ready-made capabilities, services, and tools at a reasonable rate. For instance, Amazon provides a full range of services for self-publishers and online retailers. LinkedIn has thousands of groups that allow you to easily network with others with similar interests or potential customers. Trade organizations and clubs can often provide research, contacts, and other helpful resources. Online user forums and sites such as YouTube provide extensive resources to help you learn efficiently. Relationships with "connectors," people who know lots of people and like putting them together, can give you access to huge established networks.

Conduct Small Experiments
Before investing a lot of time or energy into a project, do a quick experiment to see if you are on the right track. This might help you quickly determine, for instance, if there is interest in an idea or a market for a new product. It will allow you to learn and adjust early on, while it is generally easier, cheaper, and less embarrassing. Run your idea past a few trusted friends. Create a rough prototype. Conduct a small test or experiment. If you are on the right track, it will give you confidence to proceed. The biggest benefit of this strategy, though, is in being able to obtain feedback and catch mistakes early. While we humans generally resist criticism, this gift of information can facilitate big, fast improvements.

Go With the Flow
You've probably heard the saying from the investment world, "The trend is your friend." It's easier to go with the flow, move with the herd, walk with the wind at your back, and fish where the fishing is good.

Many very successful people have "marched to a different drummer." Doing so can be interesting and gratifying, but it generally takes more time, energy, and concentration to go against traffic.

Play Your Own Game
Criticism can be a useful tool, but some types of criticism can hold you back. Destructive criticism may undermine confidence and cause you to unnecessarily limit yourself. Some critics may have ulterior motives or fail to understand what you are trying to do. You can get so wrapped up in criticism that you end up worse off by trying to please everyone.

It may be that you are playing a different game. Know your success criteria and stick to it. Skip the rest.

Just Move Faster
When quality isn't imperative and there's no inherent joy in the activity, why not just try to move faster? Be safe—don't speed, but don't dawdle either!

Apply & Evaluate: What Do You Notice?
Experiment with a few of these acceleration strategies. Then determine:
- *How did accelerating affect your productivity?*
- *Were there other consequences—positive or negative—to accelerating?*
- *Where else could you accelerate strategically? When is slowing down a better strategy?*

Take Action: Now What?
Continue to look for places in your work and life where you can accelerate to be able to learn faster and accomplish more. Also watch for when to slow down—when quality, deep thinking, thoughtful responses, careful attention to detail, and patience count.

15 Do It Once

The Challenge: You're Buried With the Same Old Work
As Yogi Berra once declared, "It's deja-vu all over again."

The Question: How Can You Avoid Re-Creating Everything From Scratch?
Individuals, situations, and clients are unique, but some patterns, problems, and processes repeat themselves. How can you be most efficient with the routine parts of your work so you can devote better energy to the unique parts of your business?

Consider This

"Don't reinvent the wheel, just realign it."
—Anthony J. D'Angelo

"Obviously, the highest type of efficiency is that which can utilize existing material to the best advantage."
—Jawaharial Nehru

"You only live once, but if you do it right, once is enough."
—Mae West

Try This: Create Systems to Streamline Routine and Recurring Activities
Think of tasks that come up regularly in your work and life. You'll probably find that much of your activity has routine elements or includes recurring steps. In cases where the recurring process is identical, it might be set up to happen automatically. In other cases, where the process is similar, a regular system can

be designed so you only have to address the parts that change. Having a predetermined process or system can save you from having to constantly "reinvent the wheel."

"Auto-magic" Systems

Which of your activities could be automated? What might warrant an investment of time upfront so that it could subsequently happen "auto-magically?" Some examples:
- Automatic bill-paying systems
- Email autoresponders
- Reorder processes that occur at regular intervals or when inventories or supplies hit a predetermined level
- Services that automatically send birthday cards on designated dates
- Automatic "thank you" messages and offers sent to customers

Help Yourself

Some systems save time all around when they provide information and resources others can use to help themselves. Some examples:
- Frequently Asked Questions
- Online and other courses set up so a student can proceed through the materials at his or her own pace
- A system set up for kids to be able to easily make their own breakfasts and pack their own lunches

Patterns

What could you do once and then use as a pattern for further work? Set up the basic outline and then just make small adjustments or additions as needed. Some examples:
- Pre-populated forms for returning customers
- Document templates
- Babysitter directions forms
- Regular menu plans

Modules and Menus

What pieces of information or processes are needed often, but not always by everyone or not always in the same combination or order? Create modules of information that can be easily combined for tailored solutions. Some examples:
- Tailorable form letters or copy modules
- Sales information for different types of customers
- Training modules on different topics or at different levels

Checklists

For activities that require a number of routine steps, checklist systems can preserve decision-making energy, streamline processes, aid in training, and improve safety and quality. These are particularly helpful in providing a standard when you want to make sure a function performed by many different people is done consistently. Some examples:
- Packing lists
- Safety checks
- Step-by-step procedure lists

Regularly Recurring Events and Issues

Certain activities need to be done at regular intervals or in response to regularly recurring events. Holidays will come around again. Taxes will be due. Annual performance reviews are required. Set up systems to remind yourself of upcoming dates, steps to take, and information to collect as you go. Some examples:
- Track your performance and accomplishments throughout the year so you are prepared for formal performance reviews.
- Use accounting systems that organize expense information for tax preparation.
- Collect mailing list information in a way that will later easily allow you to target mailings to specific groups.
- Set up regular personal finance procedures to track spending, review and rebalance investments, and identify documents that may be discarded.

"Hand-Off" Opportunities

Systems you create may make it possible to easily hand off portions of your work to others. On a small scale, a system might allow you to delegate or outsource pieces of work. On a large scale, you might be able to create a franchise or sell a system, business, app, or software you have created.

A System for Your System

As you design your systems, don't forget to include one last step: Monitor the system periodically to make sure it is still current and working well. For example:
- Is your credit card information still current for automatic bill payments?
- Is contact information still correct on mailing lists and autoresponder messages?
- Is information used in other systems (forms, modules, FAQs, checklists) up to date?

Apply & Evaluate: What Do You Notice?

Once set up, systems can save you much time, thought, and energy. You don't have to make the same recurring decisions or expend energy redoing work that still works. Consider:

- *Which of your activities can be automated or systematized?*
- *What could you do once that would yield ongoing benefits?*
- *How can you set up systems to incorporate tailoring to make materials appear more individualized?*

Take Action: Now What?

This may all seem obvious; it's surprising that we don't do it more often. It does require some strategic thought and effort up front to set up systems. Look for ways you can leverage the work you've already done. Often, a little thought and time to take just one more step can save you considerable time over the long haul.

16   Seven Flavors Of "No"

The Challenge: Difficulty Saying "No"
In the midst of trying to keep everyone around us happy and all the balls we are juggling in the air, we may forget that most of our daily thoughts and actions involve choices—including the choice to say "No" when it's in our best interest. Even when we recognize "No" as a choice, it can be difficult to get the words out.

The Question: How Can You Actually Say "No"?
Saying "No" can be uncomfortable. We don't want to disappoint someone else. We may be afraid of the potential consequences. Sometimes it just seems harsh.

Consider This

"I'm actually as proud of the things we haven't done as the things I have done. Innovation is saying no to 1,000 things."
—Steve Jobs

"The greatest geniuses sometimes accomplish more when they work less."
—Leonardo da Vinci

Try This: Seven Flavors of "No": How to Actually Say It

All "No"s Are Not Created Equal
It can be very useful to have a repertoire of "No"s. Some situations call for "No"s that are loud and direct. Others call for soft and subtle "No"s. Here are seven different types of "No" you can pull out for different occasions, along with examples of how you might put each into words:

1) **Just "No"**

   Sometimes no explanation is needed. A simple "No" or "No, thanks" is sufficient. Don't stumble or look back. Just calmly say "No."

2) **Setting Limits**

   Sometimes we need to say "No" quickly before a problem grows bigger. For instance, we might have to say "No" to our own unproductive thinking before it takes over. (*Whoa–don't go there!*) Or we may need to react quickly to stop someone from doing something harmful to us or to themselves. (*No, don't touch that hot stove. No, don't touch me. Wait!* or *That's enough!*)

3) **Justified No**

   Sometimes "No" goes more smoothly if we give a reason. (*I can't because I'm fully booked that day. My budget doesn't allow for that.*)

   This type of No can be easiest when it's somewhat impersonal. (*It's our company policy.*) Use "No" plus a fact. (*No. That would be illegal.*)

   If you can't make it impersonal, use "I" words in your explanation. (*I'm not comfortable with that. That doesn't work for me because ... I need/want ...*)

   Resist the temptation to overexplain. State your case and stop there. (*I'm at capacity.*)

4) **Leaving the Door Open**

   Sometimes we need to say "No" for the time being, but want to keep a door open and preserve a relationship. (*I'm sorry I can't help you this time. I hope we have another opportunity. While we don't have any [openings, budget ...] at this time, we appreciate your [interest, product, idea ...].*) You may want to put a request off until another time or delay responding until you have more information. (*I need to check with my colleague. I'll think about it for a future time. I don't know. I can't tell yet.*) Be careful with this one, because it does invite the other person to come back later and try again.

5) **Negotiated No: "Yes, if ... "**

   Sometimes a "No" is a partial No and invites some negotiation. (*I can't do that, but I could do this. I could do that if we could ...*) You outline the conditions under which you could say "Yes." Perhaps the timing, scope, or something else can be negotiated so it's a "Yes, if ... " or a "Yes, when ... ". (*In order to do that, I would need ... Could it be done later? Could I start it for you or do one part? OK, I can do it if we can put off priority project x.)* With this type of "No," you try to satisfy the other person without sacrificing your own needs.

6) **Alternative No**
   The person making a request of you has some sort of need. There may be another acceptable way of taking care of it. In this case, you respond with alternatives. (*How about ... ?*) The alternatives may be specific ones (*May I suggest a better person or solution?*) or an invitation to explore other solutions (*Would you consider ... ? What if ... ?*)

7) **The Mother-In-Law or Politician No**
   There may also be times when, to preserve a relationship and avoid unnecessarily hurting feelings, it's just better not to say "No" directly, but to simply acknowledge another's opinion, suggestion, or request (*Thank you. That's interesting. I'll consider that.*), even if you plan to ignore it. Just follow these simple steps:
   Remain calm. Listen. Smile. Acknowledge. (Then ignore.)

Apply & Evaluate: What Do You Notice?
If you are uncomfortable saying "No," experiment with ways to say it that fit your situation and style. What are some other ways you could say "No" ...

   ... to be perceived as logical and reasonable?

   ... to leave the door open for further opportunities?

   ... to reject an idea or proposal while maintaining the relationship?

   ... to draw a boundary?

   ... to signal what you would say "Yes" to?

   ... to negotiate alternatives?

Next time you want to say "No," try one of these and see what happens.

Take Action: Now What?
Expand your "No" repertoire so you can conserve your own energy, preserve important relationships, and say "Yes" to priorities.

17 Tired Of SMART Goals?

The Challenge: You've Dutifully Set "SMART" Goals, But You're Stuck

You know goal setting is important. You're familiar with the research showing that people who set goals achieve more than people who don't. You also know that the smaller percentage of people who write their goals down accomplish even more.

You've been trained to write goals by using the acronym SMART. That is, goals should be Specific, Measurable, Attainable, Realistic, and Time-bound.

But you're stuck. You're not reaching your goals. You find yourself setting the same ones over and over. They're just not moving you.

Sound familiar? For some individuals and at certain times, this generally accepted "smart" method of setting goals can be frustrating or counterproductive. The format may just not fit your real objective. One may fail to meet a specific goal, yet achieve great progress in a different way. A short-term goal may be reached at the expense of other, greater, long-term goals. In extreme cases, excessive focus on goals can lead to unethical behavior or damage relationships.

The Question: What Other Ways Can You Focus Your Attention and Activities?

Goal setting works because it provides a focus for your attention and activities. The act of writing goals down strengthens your commitment to them and provides a means of accountability.

If traditional goal setting is not moving you, it may be time to try a different approach.

Try This Quick Fix First
Coaches I've worked with tap into motivation by simply adding a "Y" to the SMART goal-setting acronym, to make it "SMARTY." The "Y" is added to stand for "Yours," because the most effective goals are ones we set ourselves!

> **Consider This**
>
> *"The first step toward getting somewhere is to decide that you are not going to stay where you are."*
> —J. P. Morgan
>
> *"When it is obvious that the goal cannot be reached, don't adjust the goal, adjust the action steps."*
> —Confucius

Try This: Goal Alternatives

Here are some alternatives that can be used instead of, or in conjunction with, traditional goal-setting methods to help you focus your attention and actions. You'll notice that several of these incorporate observable, but not strictly measurable, elements. Instead of focusing solely on numbers, they focus on ways to create the thinking and behaviors that are likely, in turn, to create the results you ultimately want.

Try using these methods by setting your intentions and then watching for and taking action on opportunities and synchronicities that appear.

"Being" Focus

Instead of focusing on a specific achievement, focus on "who" you are becoming. Choose qualities or virtues to develop. Consciously try to express these consistently during a defined time period. For instance, Ben Franklin chose a virtue, such as sincerity, humility, or temperance, to work on each week.

A variation of this that has become popular in recent years is choosing a word as a theme to focus on for a time. For instance, your word for the year might be "Action" or "Gratitude."

"Purpose" Focus

Focus on your greater purpose. As you choose daily thoughts and actions, ask yourself, *"If my greater purpose is truly x, what could I be doing or thinking right now (tomorrow, next month, next year) to be in alignment with it?"* Concentrate on staying "on purpose." Let go of activities, habits, commitments, and thoughts that don't lead to its fulfillment.

Internal Motivation and Mastery Focus

For the role you have taken on, ask yourself *"What am I driven to do?"*, *"What feels like the right course of action now?"*, and *"How can I achieve excellence?"* Freedom to choose our work and methods creates internal commitment and energy, which often lead to discovery, creativity, and high-quality work.

Visualization

Visualize the end product you desire in as much detail as possible. See it. Feel it. Imagine doing it. Then, work backward. Imagine the steps that got you there. *What happened just before you arrived at the end? What happened before that?* Visualize yourself actually doing those steps. *Where, when, and how did you do them?* Increase your commitment by writing this down. Then start taking the steps with the end in mind.

Contagion Method

Hang around achievers and inspiring role-models. Be open to their positive influence and look deliberately for good, successful behaviors you can imitate. Soon, what they do will seem "normal" and you will likely begin to rise to their level.

Apply & Evaluate: What Do You Notice?

If you're stuck and traditional goal setting isn't working, try some of these alternatives. Then assess your results:
- *What kind of progress did you make?*
- *How did alternative goals affect your motivation?*
- *What other alternatives could you try to focus your attention and activities?*

Take Action: Now What?

Whether you write traditional goals or alternative ones, keep track of your key accomplishments and progress. If you're not progressing, experiment with different methods to determine what best taps into your motivation, increases your commitment, and produces the results you desire.

18. Grinding Your Gears? Take A Refresh Break

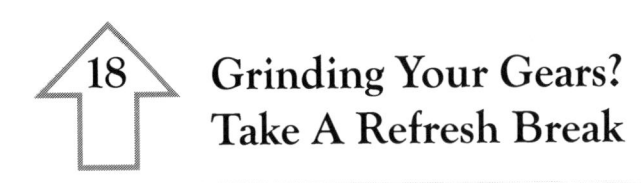

The Challenge: At Some Point, Working More Becomes Counterproductive

Under pressure to produce, we're encouraged to focus, focus, focus. At some point, we may "hit a wall."

The Question: How Can You Take a Break When You Don't Have Much Time?

Taking a break may be less about taking time and more about refreshing, refocusing, and reenergizing.

> **Consider This**
>
> *"A change is as good as a rest."*
> —Stephen King, *Hearts in Atlantis*

Try This: Refresh

Let me take a moment to encourage you to take a moment. Take a moment to breathe, to reflect, to refuel.

Build refresh breaks into your regimen to get perspective, energy, and inspiration. Use a variety of types and lengths of breaks appropriate to your needs, available time, and preferences.

If you've been working intensely for 25 minutes, for instance, break for 5 minutes to stretch, get a drink, or read something funny or inspiring. (Only check your email if you can contain it to 5 minutes!) If you've been concentrating for 90 minutes, shift to another type of activity for 30 minutes; perhaps go for a walk, take a "recess," or nap. If you only have a minute, take the opportunity to breathe deeply, stand, stretch, close your eyes, or shift to a different view as a break from the computer screen.

Several types of short refresh breaks are listed below. Experiment with different types of breaks to see what gives you the best boost. Preferences will vary by individual; some will get energized by social contact; others will crave quiet time alone.

Tech-free Break: Get away from your computer and phone for a bit—especially if you think you don't need to. Do it so you know you can. (You're neither a techno slave nor addict, right?)

Social Media Break: Social media can be a big time-waster, but a little social contact, even if virtual, can also be refreshing. Use it in limited amounts as a reward.

Human Contact Break: Even better, reach out to a friend for a real-time, two-way conversation.

Back-to-Nature Break: Enjoy some fresh air and an inspiring view. Hug a tree. Wiggle your toes in some sand. Take a dip. Lie on your back and look up at the clouds.

Self-Care Break: Do something to take good care of yourself, especially if you rarely think of doing so.

Exercise Break: A little exercise can provide big benefits to mind, body, and spirit.

Inspiration Break: Read something inspiring. View some awesome photos or art. Observe a good role model. Reflect on your life purpose. Visualize your desired outcome.

Shift Gears Break: After hard work in one area, switch to something entirely different. If you've been lifting heavy weights, rest and let those muscles rebuild.

Laugh Tracks: Watch a comic clip. Make fun. Goof around. Chuckle. Giggle. Even guffaw. Humor is not only fun, but also can relieve tension and improve your functioning. A punch line is funny because we were expecting one thing and then things take a surprising turn. This shift in thinking can break down mental barriers so new ideas can emerge.

Pit Stop: Refuel. Drink some water. Change clothes. Fix your equipment. Take care of a personal need.

"Have a Lie-Down": That's British for a nap. Artist Joan Miró, architect Buckminster Fuller, director Orson Welles, and other creatives have been known for taking short naps at all hours to refuel.

Quickie Break: Look away from your computer, book, or desk. Breathe. Release tension with a few shoulder rolls.

Daydream Break: Close your eyes. Relax. Dream.

"Recess": Get outside and play.

Celebration Break: Take a break when you complete a section of difficult work. Pat yourself on the back for small achievements that will add up to large ones.

Perspective Break: Stop. Look at your situation from a different perspective:
- *How important is this anyway?*
- *How much will it matter in five years? One year? One month? Tomorrow?*
- *How does this fit into the big picture? How does it appear up close?*
- *How will this look to others? Does that matter?*

Self-evaluation Break: Stop and ask yourself:
- *How am I doing?*
- *What am I doing well?*
- *What could I do differently or better?*

Stepping back to reflect on your work may be one of the most effective breaks of all. Harvard Business School researcher Francesca Gino and her colleagues found that workers who either reflected on their own performance or shared their reflections with a coworker performed 18-25% better than their colleagues who just kept working. According to Gino, "Our work shows that if we'd take some time out for reflection, we might be better off ... When we stop, reflect, and think about learning, we feel a greater sense of self-efficacy. We're more motivated and we perform better afterward."[1]

Apply & Evaluate: What Do You Notice?
Experiment with several types of refresh breaks. Notice:
- *Which type of breaks work best for you?*
- *What reenergizes you best if you only have a few minutes?*
- *How can you build breaks into your day to increase your energy and focus?*

Take Action: Now What?

Be alert to signs that you are grinding your gears; take a break to refresh and refocus.

As a manager and leader, consider the importance of refresh breaks not only for yourself, but for your team and colleagues.

19. Feeling Stressed? Under Pressure? Seven "A"s To Ease Your Way

The Challenge: Stress by Overload
These days almost everyone seems concerned about having too much to do and too little time to do it. They note the feeling of anxiety and pressure in their workplace that can easily spill over into other areas of their lives. (Ironically, the only thing worse seems to be not having enough [or enough with meaning] to do.)

The Question: How Can You Relieve the Pressure of "Too Much!"?

> **Consider This**
>
> *"We always have time enough if we will but use it aright."*
> —Goethe

Try This: Seven "A" Strategies to Ease Your Way
If you or those around you are feeling stressed, here are seven "A"s to ease your way:

Armor: Put on some mental armor to avoid taking in and taking on thoughts and problems that aren't yours, especially when there's anxiety in your environment. If we're not alert, at times we unconsciously accept fears and troubles that don't belong to us. Negativity can be "catching," but not if we don't let it in or pick it up and play with it. Be compassionate when appropriate, but also be watchful and armed to deflect negativity.

Align: In times of stress, it often helps to pause and remember what is really most important. Underlying all of our activities are values we hold dear. These values are the *Why* that keeps us going and gives our lives meaning. Take a few moments to think about your *Why*. You may be involved in the same activities as others, but for different reasons. This *Why* can give you the impetus to persist when the going gets tough.

Alternatives: Recognizing that you have choices can make tough situations easier to deal with. Consider your alternatives. *What else could you do? What other way could your challenge be approached?* We are rarely really "stuck." By simply considering the possibility of alternatives, you may discover a better way. Even if you don't, just realizing that choices exist may bring a sense of freedom that makes the current situation more tolerable.

A-list: One of the underlying factors that seems to cause the most stress is the lack of clear priorities. *Which goals are most important? Which activities are likely to produce the biggest and most sustainable results? Which mean the most to you? Which do you have the most energy for? What does the time seem right for now?* Weigh these and choose the most important items to handle for now. When you focus on these, other things often fall into place or fall away.

Anticipate: Think ahead to the ultimate result you want. Then think backward from that outcome to what needs to be done to get there. Consider potential obstacles and how they might be avoided or overcome if necessary.

Ask: Figure out what you need and want; then ask for it. When you're clear and approach someone who can deliver what you need, the way usually opens more easily. Be willing to ask for help, support, input, or feedback.

Act: Sometimes the hardest part of any undertaking is simply getting started. Take some action, even if it is small. As the proverb says, the longest journey begins with a single step. Once in motion, the next step is easier. Momentum builds. Success breeds success. So get going.

Apply & Evaluate: What Do You Notice?
With seven strategies, there's one for every day of the week. Try each one this week and then consider:
- *What worked for you?*
- *What else could you try?*
- *How could you help ease the way for others?*

Take Action: Now What?
Recognize choices you have regarding how you think and what you take on. Try out productivity strategies to find ones that work well for you.

20 Seven Ways To Decide

The Challenge: Decisions, Decisions
We make hundreds of them every day; some big, many small; some easy, some difficult.

The Question: What's the Best Way to Decide?
When you decide how to decide, consider both the importance and complexity of the decision. If you tend to make quick decisions, be sure to slow down a bit and think things through carefully when there are serious or long-term ramifications. If, on the other hand, you tend to suffer unnecessarily over decisions, push yourself to decide faster on minor ones.

When you have a variety of decision-making tools, you can choose the one that best fits the decision at hand. As with most skills, decision making will improve with practice and learning.

Consider This
> *"Everything should be made as simple as possible, but not simpler."*
> —Einstein

Try This: Seven Three-Step Decision-Making Models
When you face decisions, consider using one or more of these simple three-step decision-making models.

1) **Head, Heart, Gut**
   Apply logic, feeling, and intuition by asking:
   - *What does your head say?*
   - *What does your heart say?*
   - *What does your gut say?*

This method works well for personal decisions where there's more involved than facts. Along with facts and feelings, get quiet and add a "gut" or intuition check. Notice whether love or fear is driving your decision. Are you reacting to the pressure of personalities or acting on principle? Are you open to new input, or are you simply justifying your previous decisions and actions?

2) **Best, Worst, Likely**
Research by social scientists shows that people are more likely to act to prevent loss than to achieve gains. Some of us tend to optimistically focus on the "half-full" glass, while others first see the "half-empty" glass. Balance these tendencies by considering these three questions for each of your options:
- *What's the best thing that could happen as a result?*
- *What's the worst thing that could happen?*
- *What would most likely happen?*

For instance, in evaluating investments—what's the potential upside; what's the potential downside; what's most likely? Look to put your money on the option with the largest and likeliest upside, along with the smallest and least likely downside.

3) **Criteria Weighting**
Most big decisions involve multiple factors. What's most important in yours?
1) Identify top criteria against which to evaluate your options.
2) Prioritize your top criteria. What's most important of all?
3) Weigh your options against your criteria, giving extra weight to the very top factors.

Decisions often require tradeoffs. For instance, in considering career options, one might face tradeoffs between factors such as compensation, preferred location, growth opportunities, fit with values, and work environment. Choices may be very personal. Identify what's most important to you and give that weight in your decision.

4) **3D Decision Making**
Look at your options in three dimensions. For instance, evaluate how well each would work:

- Before/During/After
- Short-term/Intermediate-term/Long-term
- From 30,000 feet/On the ground/Under the microscope
- For Shareholders/Customers/Employees
- On a National/Regional/Local basis or
- From an Operational/Financial/Sales perspective

5) **Kidder's Three Ways to Resolve Dilemmas**

In his very thoughtful book *How Good People Make Tough Choices*, Rushworth Kidder pointed out that decisions are often especially difficult when they involve choices between two types of good. For instance, in making a decision, one might need to weigh what's best for individuals versus what's best for the community as a whole, or balance short-term benefits versus long-term ones. If you're facing this type of decision, he offers "Three Principles for Resolving Dilemmas":
- *"Do what's best for the greatest number of people."*
- *"Follow your highest sense of principle."*
- *"Do what you want others to do to you."*[1]

6) **De Bono's PMI: Plus/Minus/Interesting**

One of the most widely used decision-making methods is the "Pros and Cons" method attributed to Benjamin Franklin. In this method, one makes two columns on a sheet of paper, labels one "Pros" and the other "Cons," and then lists the pluses and minuses for each option under consideration.

Thinking expert Edward de Bono supplements this simple tool with a third column, "Interesting," where one lists other factors to consider. Doing so often opens up additional ideas and alternative solutions. Using this tool, then, one asks:
- *What are the pluses of this option?*
- *What are the minuses?*
- *What's interesting about it?*[2]

Don't be surprised if you generate further and better options using the process.

7) **Alternative Decision Making**

We often get stuck thinking a decision means choosing between two (or more) prescribed options. *Yes/No. Either/Or. Black/White.*

Are you limiting yourself unnecessarily? Consider adding some color and stirring it up:
- **Think in broader terms:** What is it you're really after? If you think in broader terms, instead of either/or, you might be able to have

both. For example, consider the saying, "You can't have your cake and eat it, too." What if you just wanted the memory of the cake? Take a photo and enjoy a slice.
- **Reframe:** Change the question and then look for an entirely different answer. Trying to decide between keeping your full-time job and being a stay-at-home mom? Ask instead, "How can I both contribute to family finances and have the flexibility to spend quality time with my kids?" That might open up an entirely new range of options, from job-sharing to entrepreneurship to a change of careers.
- **Flip a coin:** Can't decide? Don't want to? Maybe you don't have to. This doesn't mean avoidance, though; "Not to decide" is usually actually a decision to stay with the status quo. When any decision is better than no decision or an inconsequential choice simply has to be made, pick any method—even a random method like flipping a coin or throwing a dart. There, you've got a decision. Move forward and don't look back.

Apply & Evaluate: What Do You Notice?
Experiment with these methods and notice what happens:
- *What types of decisions do you face most often? Which methods work best for you?*
- *How can you improve the quality of your decisions?*
- *How can you improve your decision-making speed?*

Take Action: Now What?
Choose decision-making methods purposefully. With practice, your confidence will increase.

21. Beyond SWOT: Five Simple Strategy Models

The Challenge: Stale Strategic Planning
Strategy is essential for the long-term success of any venture, but leaders often get into strategic planning ruts, going through the motions in perfunctory, required annual exercises.

The Question: Besides "SWOT," What Strategic Tools Can You Use?
One of the most widely used strategic planning tools is "SWOT," in which four factors are examined:
- Strengths
- Weaknesses
- Opportunities
- Threats

While SWOT is a relatively easy and useful process, in this era of increasingly fast change and complexity, it may be time to supplement your current strategic planning methods.

Consider This

"You read a book from the beginning to the end. You run a business the opposite way. You start with the end, and then you do everything you must to reach it."
—Harold Geneen

"You've got to think about 'big things' while you're doing small things, so that all the small things go in the right direction."
—Alvin Toffler

"The best way to predict the future is to create it."
—Peter Drucker

Try This: Five Simple Strategy Models

Enhance your strategic planning process by adding these five options to your strategic toolbox:

1) **SOAR: Moving Toward Your Preferred Future**

    SOAR is an alternative to SWOT. This "Appreciative Inquiry" tool, first developed by David Cooperrider and Suresh Srivastva at Case Western Reserve University, asks questions to value the best of "what is" and envision "what might be":
    - **Strengths:** *What are our greatest assets?*
    - **Opportunities:** *What are the best market opportunities?*
    - **Aspirations:** *What is our preferred future?*
    - **Results:** *What are the measurable results?*[1]

    While SWOT is generally used as a "tops-down" tool, SOAR works well to involve multiple levels and functional areas of an organization. Users like the positive, collaborative approach that opens thinking, encourages engagement, and creates energy. While looking for ways to capitalize on Strengths and Opportunities, it also guides planners toward implementation by looking at how to achieve Aspirations and Results.

2) **PEST: Big Picture Factors**

    Supplement your SWOT or SOAR analysis with one that considers big picture factors. PEST helps you analyze how Political, Economic, Social, and Technological factors and trends might affect your environment. Examples of such factors include:

    Political:
    - Global events
    - Change of government
    - Legislation

    Economic:
    - Economic cycles
    - Interest rates, tax issues
    - Industry issues and trends

    Social
    - Demographics
    - Lifestyle trends
    - Attitudes

Technological:
- Impact of new technology
- Technological solutions
- Disruptive technologies

The PEST tool was first suggested by Harvard professor Francis Aguilar. Others have enhanced it by adding Legal, Environmental, and Ethics factors, as well as Local, National, and Global factors to create acronyms such as PESTLE, STEEP or LoNGPESTLE.

3) **Perspectives: Multidimensional Views**
As you develop your strategy, step away and examine it from multiple perspectives. For instance, consider different **Stakeholder** perspectives:
- Investors
- Customers
- Employees
- Community
- Suppliers

Other dimensions might also be considered, such as:
- **Timeframe:** Short-term–Mid-term–Long-term
- **Geographical:** Local–Regional–National or Regional–National–Global
- **Vertical/Hierarchical:** Implementers–Managers–Executives
- **Lateral:** My Department–Department A–Department B

4) **Critical Success Factors: Essentials for Results**
Critical Success Factors are the ones most necessary for the success of a mission or project. They are what you must be, do, or have to be successful. The concept was developed by D. Ronald Daniel of McKinsey & Company and later refined by John F. Rockart from MIT's Sloan School of Management.

After analyzing your situation and clarifying your goals, cull your findings down to identify 4–8 factors that are most critical to producing results. Your CSFs should represent an achievable and complete summary of the essentials needed to reach your goals.

For instance, if one's goal is to launch a successful information product, the CSFs might be to reach an **identifiable market** with a **high-quality presentation** of **unique content** through **active promotion**, **prospect engagement**, and a **wide distribution network**.

If one's goal were to change jobs, the CSFs might be a **well-defined objective**, **timely targeted research resources**, an **active network** to identify relevant opportunities, **standout career marketing materials**, **sharp interviewing skills**, and a **strong personal support system**.

5) **Scenario Planning Plus: The Change Cascade**
Major change used to be followed by ample periods of adjustment and "rest." With today's technological advances and instant information flow, changes are occurring more quickly and frequently. While "10-year plans" may have seemed reasonable in the past, in some fields it's now difficult to even project 3-5 years out. Additionally, our decisions and strategies often result in a cascade of further decisions and "unintended consequences."

To prepare for these challenges, it's important to look past the current decision at hand. If we're in the midst of a change, it will not be the last one. Look ahead to predict potential changes after this one.

Add an extra column when you do "Scenario Planning" or add an extra "twig" to the branches when you draw "Decision Trees." For instance, identify possible scenarios and their potential outcomes—the range of results, risks, rewards, challenges, and opportunities of each. Then consider the potential resulting scenarios of each option: What might happen next after that? What might happen longer-term?

Scenario	Plan	Outcomes	Potential Resulting Scenarios

While it's impossible to predict exactly what will happen, including this process in your planning increases your chances of anticipating changes, leveraging opportunity, and minimizing risk longer-term.

Apply & Evaluate: What Do You Notice?
As you prepare for strategic planning, consider:
- *What's the most appropriate timeframe for your organization's strategic planning?*
- *Which tools are most appropriate for your situation?*
- *Who needs to be included in the planning process?*

Take Action: Now What?

As you translate your strategy into concrete plans, make decisions, and move forward, consider other organizational processes that can be enhanced, updated, streamlined, or simplified.

22. The Single Most-Effective Productivity Strategy

The Challenge: Making Sure the Right Things Get Done

The Question: How Can You Make the Very Best Use of Your Time?

Consider This

> *"Action expresses priorities."*
> —Mahatma Gandhi

Try This: High-Impact Activities First

All Activities Are Not Equal
Remember the 80/20 Rule? It applies in many realms, including your personal productivity. You may be a very busy person, but all of your activities aren't created equal. About 20% of your activities probably produce about 80% of your results. We'll call those your "High-Impact Activities."

Determine Your Highest-Impact Activities
Start by thinking "big picture." Consider your overarching purpose and most significant goals. Using a longer-term time horizon (e.g. yearly or more, quarterly, or monthly, depending on your role), ask:
- *If you could only achieve a few things during this period, which would be most important?*
- *Which accomplishments would have the greatest overall impact?*

Write down your three "Big Picture" Highest-Impact Accomplishments:
1)
2)
3)

Then consider a more immediate timeframe (e.g. monthly, weekly, daily).

Right now, which 1–3 activities will lead you most directly to those High-Impact Accomplishments?

Write down your three "Daily" Highest-Impact Activities:
1)
2)
3)

Schedule Your Highest-Impact Activities First!
Keep High-Impact Accomplishments and Activities at the forefront for all of your planning:
- As you write your yearly, monthly, and weekly goals, identify and focus on the Highest-Impact Accomplishments and Activities that will move you most directly toward reaching them.
- Every evening, write down your 1–3 Highest-Impact Activities for the next day. Schedule these as the first activities in your day.
- Post them where they will be visible to you throughout the day.
- Let other less important activities work around them.

High Impact First Today!
Work on your Highest-Impact Activity first thing each day. Your productivity will increase immensely if you undertake the most important activity BEFORE other things come up. (Yes, this may mean putting off all but the most urgent email in the morning!)

But ...
... **I'm NOT a morning person!** If you are "not a morning person," put your Highest-Impact Activity off until your personal "Prime Time," your most productive work time, ONLY IF you can firmly schedule it and avoid interruptions later. Otherwise, it's likely the day will get away from you.

... **what about my colleague's urgent project?** If something "urgent" comes up, test it to be sure it is truly urgent and at least as important as your Highest-Impact Activity before "bumping" your priority. If you must stray, immediately plan a time to get back to your Highest-Impact Activity.

... I'll just do something easy first to warm up. Often the Highest-Impact Activity is also a difficult one. If it seems overwhelming, try breaking the activity down into smaller steps and taking it on one step at a time. Often the momentum from a smaller action will drive you forward.

... I think I'll wait until a better time. For some activities, especially those that involve others, right timing can be imperative. If you find yourself putting something off until "a better time," test that impulse. How likely are things to improve if you wait? Sometimes waiting until the time is right or more information is available can make a big difference. Often, though, it's an excuse to procrastinate.

Try this strategy and see how much you accomplish!

Keep a log, noting your progress on Highest-Impact Activities. Review it regularly, noting successes, as well as anything that may have distracted you. Celebrate your successes and make any needed adjustments to improve your record. Evaluate your overall results on a regular basis to know where your efforts are paying off; then adjust your High-Impact Activities list as needed.

Apply & Evaluate: What Do You Notice?

Identify your Highest-Impact Activities. Schedule your top one first thing in your day for 3-5 days. Then notice:
- *How did your overall productivity level change?*
- *What would be the impact if you continued to do this every day?*
- *What pulled you away or might distract you from your High-Impact Activities? What can you do to maintain High-Impact Focus?*

Take Action: Now What?

It's likely that everything on your "to do" lists won't get done. Make sure the most important activities get your priority time and best attention.

For many people, adjusting their "to do" list and schedule to guarantee focus on their highest results-producing activities will dramatically improve their productivity. Try it yourself for a month or so. If you stumble, keep going. Make adjustments to make the strategy work for you. If you find it beneficial, consider how the strategy might be applied within your team to achieve greater overall productivity and results.

CREATIVITY & INNOVATION

23 Help! I'm Not Creative!

The Challenge: In an Era That Demands Innovation, You're Lost
Innovation is "in." Due to economic trends, technological development, and globalization, coasting is not an option. At the same time, opportunities have never been greater for those who can innovate successfully.

Innovation involves much more than creativity, but it starts there. What if you're not creative?

The Question: HOW Are You Creative?
Researchers have found that 98% of five-year-olds—but only 2% of adults over 25—are "highly creative."[1]

You had it once. *Where did that little creative genius go?*

To revive your native genius and develop your creative capacity, start by exploring what kind of Creative you are.

> ### Consider This
> *"The action of the child inventing a new game with his playmates; Einstein formulating a theory of relativity; the housewife devising a new sauce for the meat; a young author writing his first novel; all of these are, in terms of our definition, creative, and there is no attempt to set them in some order of more or less creative."*
> —Carl R. Rogers, On Becoming a Person

Try This: Find Your Creativity Combination

Creativity Comes in Many Flavors
When we say "creative," what type of person do you picture first? Perhaps a contemporary painter or a jazz musician? Or a "mad scientist" in the lab? Some

of the most obvious expressions of creativity are found in the arts and sciences, but there's potential to express creativity in every field.

> *"Deals are my art form. Other people paint beautifully on canvas or write wonderful poetry. I like making deals, preferably big deals. That's how I get my kicks."*
> —Donald Trump

Your Unique Creativity Combination
Your creative capacity comes from a combination of factors that form, activate, drive, and sustain it. Creativity combines with your motivation, interests, intelligences, style, personal qualities, and experience to form a powerful, unique Creativity Combination.

Motivation: Where You're Driven to Apply Your Creativity
We are usually most creative in activities we love. Consider:
- *What do you love to do or think about?*
- *What are you naturally curious about?*
- *What do you get so "into" that you "lose yourself" and lose track of time?*
- *What do you care about most?*

The willingness to concentrate and persist is a key factor in creative endeavors. You are more likely to dedicate your best energy and persist in spite of failures if it's for something you deeply care about.

Interests: Where You Like to Play
Think back to the playground or playtime when you were a child. How were you creative then? Did you invent games? Make up your own rules? Build "forts"? Act out stories? Start clubs? Draw on the sidewalk or make mud pies? Imagine other worlds? Come up with moneymaking schemes? What did you like to play with? Look for hints there to find your natural creative territory.

As adults, we usually gravitate toward and develop expertise in activities that involve one or more of these four areas: **People, Idea, Data, Things**. Each area provides a distinct realm for creativity. Consider, for instance, Benjamin Franklin and the American Founding Fathers being creative with ideas when they worked out a system for democracy. In pioneering social media with Facebook, Mark Zuckerberg was creative with people. Thomas Edison, who accumulated more than a thousand U.S. patents, was creative with things. Billy Beane, former manager of the Oakland Athletics, portrayed in the movie *Moneyball*, showed creativity with data by looking at player statistics in a new way.

Multiple Intelligences: Your Kind of "Smarts"

Your natural combination of different types of intelligence also contributes to how and where you might be most successful creatively. Howard Gardner, professor of psychology at Harvard University, identified seven different types of intelligence: linguistic, logical-mathematical, bodily-kinesthetic, visual-spatial, musical, interpersonal, and intrapersonal (and later added two more—naturalistic and existential). According to Gardner, each individual has a unique combination of these intelligences.[2] To find yours, start by considering: *What kinds of problems can you solve? What are you good at? What kind of "smarts" do you have?*

Methods: How You Go About Creative Work

Depending on our natural thinking preferences, we may go about our creativity in very different ways. Some of us get energy and ideas from outside of ourselves, while others draw best from inside. Some people may do their best creative work, then, by being out in the world and bouncing ideas off of others. Others may do best by themselves with quiet for deep concentration. The creative process may look very different for these different types.

Practical vs. Conceptual Creativity: The Form Your Solutions Take

Are you drawn more toward ideas and concepts or toward practical solutions? Your answer may determine the type of creative problems you are inclined to take on and the form of your creative output. For instance, one music teacher might come up with creative ways to practice scales, where another might combine art, history, literature, and music in a multi-disciplinary program. One marketer might devise a new three-step customer follow-up process, while another might imagine a whole new product line.

Creativity and Innovation Process: When You Shine

In the process of creativity and innovation, ideas go through several stages—Idea Generation, Evaluation, Activation, and Refinement. Some people shine during the "wild idea" stage, while others contribute most naturally to designing practical solutions, putting the pieces together, or refining them. All of these are necessary to bringing creative ideas to fruition.

Qualities: Your Character Strengths

Your personal character qualities also contribute to how you show your creativity. Certain characteristics are particularly associated with creativity—openness, ability to see things differently, courage, and curiosity, for instance. What else do you bring to the creative process? Discipline? Persistence? Compassion? Resourcefulness? Initiative?

Creative Fodder: What You Have Experienced
Lastly, everything you have taken in provides material for creative work—your knowledge, the places you have visited, the people you have known, the books you have read, the art you have seen.

Apply & Evaluate: What Do You Notice?
Put together the pieces to explore your Creativity Combination:
- *In what type of activities can you most naturally express your creativity?*
- *What personal qualities, abilities, and experiences enhance your creativity?*
- *What is your creative style?*

Take Action: Now What?
Knowing your Creativity Combination prepares you to find places to contribute in the innovation process. Explore and develop your creativity by experimenting with idea generation methods and other creativity tools. Claim your creativity and practice it. Give that little creative genius a place to come out and play!

24 Ignite Your Creative Capacity

The Challenge: The Creative Mystique
A certain mystique surrounds creativity. We read of scientific discoveries and magical "aha" moments. We see wildly creative artists and wonder how they come up with their ideas. You may come away feeling creativity is either something you have or you don't. Even if you feel you were blessed with some creative ability, you may feel you're not nearly as creative as others or as you'd like to be.

The Question: How Can You Learn to Be More Creative?

> **Consider This**
>
> *"Talent can't be taught, but it can be awakened."*
> —Wallace Stegner

Try This: Ignite Your Creative Capacity
No matter where you feel you're starting from on the creativity spectrum, it's possible to increase your creativity.

Start With a Creative Attitude
If you were once a kid, there's a 98% chance you are creative. We'll assume here that you're part of the 98%. Start by claiming your innate creativity. It's still there underneath all of your adult habits, rules, and expertise.

Borrow some preschoolers. Notice how they approach life. Watch them play. Left to their own devices, they're curious and unencumbered by "right answers." They try stuff. If it doesn't work, they try something else. They don't worry about being "wrong." They ask, ask, ask. (Preschoolers ask an average of about 100 questions a day.¹) They don't worry too much about what others think. They look forward to learning and growing.

Maturity, experience, and orderliness have their pluses, so don't throw that all away. You don't have to be silly, unless you want to be. When you want to be creative, adopt childlike qualities such as playfulness, curiosity, and freedom. As you would a child, encourage yourself without self-criticism to explore, learn, make mistakes, and learn some more.

Recognize Your Creativity Combination
We often associate creativity with artistry. True, most artists naturally express much creativity, but creativity can be expressed in any field or profession. Depending on a number of other factors, you will express your creativity in your own unique way. As noted in the previous article, your motivation, interests, abilities, style, personal qualities, and experience all combine to produce your unique Creativity Combination.

Understand the Creative Process
Creativity often appears to just appear. That magical "Eureka" moment happens. Ideas flow. Underlying all of that, though, are common processes that occur either consciously or subconsciously—usually over time. For instance, that idea that emerged in an "aha" moment probably had been percolating underneath the surface for some time. Alternatively, it may have come from a deliberate process of problem identification, idea generation, idea evaluation, testing, and adjusting.

We can generate ideas more easily by keeping thought open and not judging them or identifying complications too soon. Afterward, there's a time to evaluate, select, and refine your ideas. By understanding the distinction between these modes and separating them during your process, you'll improve your creative output.

Acquire Creative Tools and Techniques
There are many techniques that can be used to generate ideas. You probably have experience with at least one of these—brainstorming. Upgrade your skill with that popular technique (See *Should Brainstorming Be Banned?*, p. 109) and learn additional ones. For instance, look at your problem with "fresh eyes" by asking a five-year-old or a taxi driver or (figuratively) an alien to solve it. Or check it out from different angles as if you were operating a video camera.

Look for Creative Opportunities
Watch for opportunities to apply your creativity—in your home, in your work, in your play, or just because. *How can things be improved? What bugs you? What are*

you curious about? What is being assumed and how could you look at things differently? These provide clues to creative opportunities. Carry a notebook or use your mobile device to collect ideas as they occur to you.

Go With Your Flow
Choose projects you really care about. You'll be much more motivated to persist.

Practice, Practice, Practice
As with any other skill, your creative skill will improve and evolve with practice.

Hang Out With Creative Cats
Unless we're consciously resisting it, we humans often take on characteristics of the people around us. Make that work for you by seeking out Creatives of different types. Take an artist to lunch. Watch a breakthrough educator in action. Visit a lab. Rub elbows with entrepreneurs. Ask a five-year-old for advice.

Set Up to Create
Creativity doesn't always appear on command, but it does help to schedule specific time to work on creative projects. A physical space that is conducive to creating will also help, whether that entails a comfy chair, an inspiring view, white noise, or classical music. Have the necessary tools handy. Writers and other creators often have a little ritual they use to "invoke the Muse"—that is, to get their creative juices flowing. Figure out a time, space, and routine that will stimulate and support your creativity.

Apply & Evaluate: What Do You Notice?
Begin by looking for ways you can develop your creativity:
- *What can you do to shift into creative mode?*
- *What problems can you take on for practice?*
- *How can you set up your network, schedule, workspace, and routine to support your creative efforts?*

Take Action: Now What?
Start where you are and actively expand your creative capacity. Take on a creative mindset. Play with additional tools and techniques detailed in following articles. Experiment with your routines and workspace. Identify opportunities to make both small and significant improvements in your work and life and celebrate the results!

25 When To Bother With Creativity

The Challenge: Thinking Outside-the-Box Takes Energy
You've got a lot on your plate. You've been encouraged to "think outside the box" when problem-solving. Sounds great, but you need to be efficient.

The Question: When Is Creativity the Answer?
The Answer: Not always.

> **Consider This**
>
> *"I think and think for months and years. Ninety-nine times the conclusion is false. The hundredth time I am right. It's not that I'm so smart, it's just that I stay with problems longer."*
> —Albert Einstein
>
> *"Perhaps the single most reliable finding in our studies is that creative work takes a long time. With all due apologies to thunderbolts, creativity is not a matter of milliseconds, minutes, or even hours—but of months, years, and decades."*
> —H. E. Gruber and S. N. Davis, *Inching Our Way Up Mt. Olympus*

Try This: Choose the Most Efficient Thinking Process
Select a fitting approach to the problem at hand, considering the type and level of opportunity and the importance of the outcome. Sometimes creativity, complexity, and quality count. Other times, it makes sense to expedite, simplify, or do something well enough for the time being. Will expending extra energy or applying a different process make a difference? Preserve your energy to be able to apply it where it counts most.

Choose the Optimal Type of Thinking

We often approach situations with a "default" thinking process, the one we go to if we don't consciously reset it to something else.

Our default thinking process may be a result of our natural wiring, our training, or the culture in which we're operating. For instance, lawyers are trained to always look for risks. Creative types often automatically go "outside the box." Some of us like to forge ahead with the first adequate answer we think of, while others like to keep options open while they search for the ultimate solution. Some look for what's wrong or what doesn't fit. Some like to get input from many people.

None of these inclinations are good or bad per se. Specific approaches can be more or less effective for certain types of activities, though. Let's look at some different modes of thinking.

Divergent vs. Convergent Thinking

Divergent and convergent thinking are two distinct types of thinking fitting two distinct types of situations. Picture divergent thinking as opening a door and convergent thinking as closing it.

Traditional education has been more oriented toward convergent thinking, which seeks to select, judge, compare, and decide. Thinking in this mode, we look for what's wrong, what doesn't fit, and what won't work.

Divergent thinking, on the other hand, the type associated more with creativity, seeks to build and create. Thinking in this mode, we look for what's good and what's possible.

Both types of thinking are useful. To be most productive, we need to select and apply the most effective type of thinking for the task and then switch modes efficiently as needed. For instance, in addressing creative problems or designing something new, it's most effective to use "open door" divergent thinking techniques, such as brainstorming, to explore and generate ideas. Then, at a certain point, convergent "close the door" thinking is needed to judge, decide, and move ahead.

Creative Thinking: When Is It Worth It?

While creativity can be stimulated by using a variety of thinking tools and processes, it may require a significant investment of time, thought, and energy. Not every problem calls for a creative solution. To determine if creativity is needed, first ask yourself:

What's the potential benefit of pursuing a creative solution?
In theory, creativity can improve anything. It can aid in either fixing what's "broke" or in inventing something totally new. For many, the process can be fun and interesting, too. But is it worth it? Ask yourself:
- *Is solving this problem important enough to warrant devoting time and creative energy to it?*
- *How large or significant are the potential benefits of a solution?*

Is another response more appropriate?
Creativity may not be the most appropriate response to your problem. For instance, alternative responses might include:
- **Acceptance**: *Is the problem worth addressing at all?*
- **Simplicity**: *Can your problem be solved simply?*
- **Structure:** *Can your problem be structured so that a standard or existing solution will address most of it?* Then you can just address the exceptional parts.
- **Redefinition:** *Are you addressing the right problem?* For example, are you trying to solve a product problem when the real underlying problem is a "people problem," such as a communication problem, a training problem, a reluctance to address conflict, or a need for different personnel?

When It's Worth It
When your problem does call for creativity:

1) **Switch gears.** Get ready to start with some divergent thinking.

2) **Make time and space.** Allow for time and space to carry out the Creative Process: Define the Problem, Generate Ideas, Evaluate Ideas, Implement the Plan, Evaluate and Refine the Plan.

3) **Involve people who really care about finding a solution.**

4) **Use effective creativity tools and processes.** Increase the likelihood that solutions will emerge and evolve by using a variety of effective creativity tools and processes to explore and generate ideas.

Apply & Evaluate: What Do You Notice?
Consider your thinking processes for a variety of types of problems. Notice:
- *What's your default approach?*
- *If you regularly collaborate with someone else, what's their default approach?*
- *How could you guide your team to the most efficient processes?*

Take Action: Now What?
Deliberately switch thinking gears to solve problems more efficiently. Continue to add to your thinking toolkit.

26 Creative Opportunity List

The Challenge: It's Hard to Be Creative On Command

The Question: How Can You Find Creative Ideas and Opportunities?

Consider This

> *"Make it a habit to keep on the lookout for novel and interesting ideas that others have used successfully. Your idea needs to be original only in its adaptation to the problem you are working on."*
> —Thomas Edison

> *"We are all faced with a series of great opportunities —brilliantly disguised as insoluble problems."*
> —John W. Gardner

Try This: Build a Creative Opportunity List

Keep a Creative Opportunity List—a list of problems that would benefit from creative solutions, ideas from one realm that could be applied to another, and creative ideas to explore further.

Develop a Creative Mindset:

Be on the constant lookout for ideas to develop. Be curious. Ask questions. Explore. Wonder "Why?" or "Why not?" Notice how things work—or don't. Expose yourself to new people, ideas, and perspectives. Be observant. Play. You'll be surprised at what comes to you when you are alert and open to creative opportunities.

Collect Ideas

Always keep a small notebook, a notes "app," a pad of post-its, or a few blank 3x5 cards with you to record ideas as they come to you so you can work with them later.

Allocate Time for Creative Focus

Identify a specific time to think creatively. For instance, allocate 10 minutes every morning or evening to generate new ideas. Meet a creativity partner for lunch once a week. Make your showering or shaving time "idea time." Did you know that the "groggy" time between sleep and awake is a time when ideas often come together? (Make sure you keep a pad of paper and pen on your night-stand!)

Invite Inspiration

During your creative time, keep your mind open to welcome inspiration. Get outside and take a walk. Block out anxious thoughts. Relax. Breathe. Daydream. Write freely in a journal without stopping to edit or immediately reread what you wrote.

Explore

Stimulate your thinking by exploring new territory. Take a different route home. Wander the mall. Check out an art gallery. Listen to a different genre of music. Talk with someone of a different generation. Watch a different news channel. Thumb through a magazine you've never picked up before. Go someplace new for lunch. Surf the net. Exercise your curiosity. Ask questions. As you explore, keep you eyes, ears, and mind open.

Record Obvious Opportunities

Notice and keep a list of obvious opportunities for improvement or creative solutions.

Look for Unfulfilled Needs

Search deliberately. What do you and others need to make your life or business better? What would make you or your customers or employees happier? More satisfied? More successful? Less stressed? Put yourself in the others' shoes. Ask. Listen. Observe.

Embrace Problems

Be alert to things that "bug" you and others. Note annoyances. Gather complaints. Notice frustrations and worries. Spot things that aren't working.

What's wasting your time, money, or energy? What's too complicated or inefficient? These are clues to hidden opportunities for creative solutions.

Keep an Eye on the Future
Be a trend-watcher. What's changing or likely to change? How will new technology open up new opportunities? What will people need or want in the future? What old solutions can be adapted in new ways?

Apply & Evaluate: What Do You Notice?
If you don't already have one, start a Creative Opportunity List. Then consider:
- *Are you getting more ideas when you are deliberately looking for them?*
- *How are you getting most of your ideas?*
- *Now that you have a list of creative opportunities, what's the next step?*

Take Action: Now What?
Keep adding to your Creative Opportunity List. From time to time, go back and look through your ideas. You may detect patterns or see ways to combine them. Choose a few ideas that intrigue you and take steps to develop them.

27 Should Brainstorming Be Banned?

The Challenge: Bad Brainstorming Behaviors
"Let's get together and brainstorm some ideas." Sounds harmless enough, right?

When it's done well, brainstorming produces loads of ideas that can be culled and massaged to yield a few great ones. But often participants dread it, are skeptical of its effectiveness in producing actionable ideas, and see it is a colossal waste of time.

What goes wrong? A few outspoken participants hog the floor. Subordinates cater to what they think the highest-ranking person in the room wants. The discussion goes off on wild tangents or just becomes a rehash. Interesting ideas might be generated, but then nothing happens.

The Question: How Can Your Group Generate More and Better Ideas?
There's no need to ban brainstorming. Boost your results by incorporating group and idea generation best practices.

Consider This
"The way to get good ideas is to get lots of ideas, and throw the bad ones away."
—Linus Pauling

Try This: Better Brainstorming
A well-designed idea generation process can make all the difference.

Draft a Potent Participant Combination
Select participants with contribution and collaboration in mind. Invite people with genuine interest in the topic and motivation to find solutions. Include members with different experience, roles, and perspectives.

Keep the group to a size conducive to participation—usually eight or fewer. You'll want a group large enough to inspire a variety and volume of ideas, but small enough that participants feel their contributions are needed and important.

Consider changing the group membership occasionally to keep it fresh. For instance, bring in an expert or, conversely, bring in a smart, innovative person who knows little about your topic. It will be easy for them to get "outside the box," since they don't know where the box is.

For major brainstorming meetings, consider designating a Recorder to capture all the ideas and a Facilitator, whose role is to manage the process, but not contribute ideas. A Facilitator sets up the space, manages the time, guides the group to work together effectively, uses tools to stimulate thinking, ensures that ideas are recorded, summarizes decisions, and obtains agreement on next steps, so you and your participants can focus on the creative part.

Lead With a Productive Question
Choose a topic that 1) warrants the group's time, 2) would benefit from a creative approach, and 3) is one you're likely to act on afterward. Pose a question that's broad enough to expand thinking, but specific enough to produce practical ideas. Ensure you're addressing the underlying issue by articulating "What we really want is ... ." Keep asking "Why?" until you get to the root reasons. Begin your brainstorming question with "How might we ... ?" to open thinking. Circulate the main question in advance to give people a chance to mull it over.

Get Off to a Good Start
Set up for creative collaboration. A distraction-free space away from everyday tasks is ideal. Arrange the group in a semicircle facing "the problem" together. Allow room for participants to move around. Incorporate visuals and symbols to trigger humor, playfulness, and inspiration.

Warm up creative thinking with a funny cartoon or video related to your topic. Provide materials to collect and develop ideas, including materials for individual use—paper, colored notecards, or "backs of envelopes"—as well as materials to build on others' ideas, such as colored markers, sticky notes, white boards, or flip charts.

You're probably familiar with the basic rules of brainstorming: 1) Go for a volume of ideas. 2) Anything goes. 3) Don't judge ideas yet. Briefly review these guidelines with the group.

To prompt a greater and faster flow of ideas, set goals (*Let's try to generate 20 ideas ...*) and time limits (*... in 10 minutes*). If you're in the midst of an idea cascade, you can always extend the time.

Individual Thinking First
To make the most of the group's collective thinking, begin with individual idea generation. Before opening up group discussion, give individuals a few minutes of quiet to think and jot down ideas. This helps quieter participants develop their ideas enough to speak up without getting drowned out by more extroverted types. It also prevents the capable-but-lazy from simply drafting on others' efforts. If there is a big difference in experience or level, ask the higher-ranking and more experienced participants to hang back initially to encourage others to contribute fresh and unbiased ideas.

Stimulate Ideas
Use creativity techniques to stimulate ideas:

> **Building:** "Hitchhike" or "piggyback" on ideas that have already been expressed. Create variations. Keep the conversation flowing with questions such as "What else could we do along the same lines?" or "What could be added or altered?"
>
> **Shifting:** When building slows down, switch gears to go in a different direction. Ask, "How can we look at this differently?"
>
> **Restart:** Pause, repeat, or reframe the question. Alternate between individual and group idea generation.
>
> **Improvise:** Draw out ideas with an improvisor's technique. No matter what the person before you says, say "Yes, and ... "
>
> **Challenge assumptions:** Identify and remove presumed limits.
>
> **Try on different hats:** Look at your problem as different stakeholders or totally unrelated parties would. For instance, how would your customer or a five-year-old view your situation?

Ideas tend to come in bursts and improve as you go, so keep pushing to get past the obvious.

Make It Useful
Nothing is more demotivating to brainstorming participants than investing their time and energy and then seeing nothing happen as a result. Make sure to define and execute an appropriate follow-up process. For a simple issue, you might evaluate ideas immediately and make a decision. For more complex and important issues, you might let the ideas simmer for a short time, provide a means to supplement them, and then get back together to refine, combine, cull, adjust, evaluate, and choose ideas for specific follow-up.

Apply & Evaluate: What Do You Notice?
As you try out these strategies in brainstorming sessions, pay attention to your results. Consider:
- *In setting up your group and space, what works best to draw out the best participation?*
- *Which techniques stimulate the most and best ideas?*
- *How can you make the most of your idea output?*

Take Action: Now What?
Now that you've generated lots of ideas, develop and use effective processes to evaluate them. (Try *Moving Ideas Ahead: The BRAIN Process*, p. 188.) As a leader, consider ways to continue to expand and hone your own facilitation skills, as well as your group's collaboration and creativity skills.

28. Backward Bugs: Turn Complaints And Annoyances Into Solutions

The Challenge: Complaints and Annoyances
Is something bugging you or your customers? Got complaints?

The Question: How Can You Turn Complaints and Annoyances Into Solutions?
If you can move beyond annoyance, you may be able to convert these "bugs" into opportunities.

> **Consider This**
>
> *"Customers can't always tell you what they want,*
> *but they can always tell you what's wrong."*
> —Carly Fiorina
>
> *"Within the problem is the solution to the problem."*
> —Chinese proverb

Try This: Reverse a Bug
Take a "bug" and turn it around. Whatever it is that bugs you or your customer is what you don't want. What is it you *do* want, then?

If you can identify exactly what's bugging you and reverse it, you may be able to transform it into a positive either of two ways. A "Backward Bug" provides either the words to make a productive request or a topic for innovation.

Shifting From Complaint to Request
While a complaint may simply be a means of venting, it can also be a sign that someone cares enough about an issue to expend energy on it. If handled

skillfully, it might yield useful information and lead to positive action. Can you reverse the complaint to turn it into a request that can be acted upon?

Give yourself and others a hand to shift from complaint to request by asking questions such as:
- *What are you requesting?*
- *What would your ideal situation be?*
- *What would be acceptable? What would satisfy you?*
- *What do you really care about here?*

If you or they can't articulate an answer to these, probe further to clarify or put forth a proposal to elicit a response. For example, *"Do you mean ... ?"* or *"What if ... , would that work?"*

Alleviate frustration and pave the way for solutions by recasting complaints as requests.

Profit From Annoyances: Ideas for Innovation

For entrepreneurs, intrapreneurs, and creatives of all kinds, annoyances can be gifts. "Bugs" are opportunities looking for solutions. If it's "bugging" you, it's probably bugging someone else, too. Who would that be? How could you turn that annoyance into a solution?

Follow These Five Steps to "Reverse a Bug":

1) List things that "bug" or frustrate you.
2) Take one and turn it into a problem to solve by reversing it. State with positive language *what you want*.
3) Ask, "How could I (or we, or they) find a way to ... (what you want)?"
4) Use that question to brainstorm ideas.
5) Choose the best ideas, refine them, and take action.

Here's an example of how this might work:
1) **Spot a bug:** *It really bugs me when I have to stand in line or wait on the phone when I want information from x business.*
2) **Reverse it**: State what you want. *I want Immediate Answers.*
3) **Ask, "How could I ... ?"**: *How could I find a way to get Immediate Answers?*
4) **Generate ideas, using that question:** Some ideas for this "bug" might be:
    - *Ask the business to contact me at a time convenient for me.*
    - *Have them notify me when there is no waiting time.*
    - *Obtain instant information from an online resource.*
    - *Pay more to obtain faster service.*
    - *Earn better attention by being a better or bigger customer.*

- *Switch to a more customer-friendly business.*
- *Set up a process to obtain needed information automatically.*

5) **Choose, refine, and act on ideas generated.**

The ideas generated above are from the perspective of the frustrated customer, who might then recognize an alternative course of action. Similarly, a business might go through this process to generate improvement ideas.

Apply & Evaluate: What Do You Notice?

When something is annoying you or a complaint comes your way, see if you can turn it into a request or a creative opportunity by reversing it:
- *What is it that you want?*
- *How could you get that?*
- *Which ideas will you try?*

Take Action: Now What?

Keep a journal or list of things that bug you. Not only can it be therapeutic to write them down, but at the same time you will be collecting innovation material!

Select items from your list and transform them into Backward Bugs to generate potential solutions. You might even invite Backward Bugs' relatives to the party: *Turn it "inside out." Flip it "upside down." Rewind it. Disassemble it. Make it go the opposite direction.* See the following article for more ways to view things differently.

29   Stuck? Change Your View

The Challenge: You're Stuck On a Problem
You've tried and tried to solve it.

The Question: How Can You See New Possibilities?
It's time to take a different approach.

Consider This

> *"When I eat a tomato I look at it the way anyone else would.*
> *But when I paint a tomato, then I see it differently."*
> —Henri Matisse

> *"A great thought begins by seeing something differently,*
> *with a shift of the mind's eye."*
> —Albert Einstein

Try This: Take a Videographer's View
As the story goes, Einstein's first step toward discovering the Theory of Relativity came as a thought experiment at age 16. In his mind, he saw himself riding on a beam of light. If you're stuck on a problem, try changing your mental view. Examine your problem from many different perspectives.

Videographer Views
Think as a Director of Photography guiding a videographer. Adjust your thinking in different ways to examine your problem from different angles, through different lenses, and under different lights. Adjust the speed and the

sound. By viewing your problem in different ways, you are likely to discover new options, questions, approaches, and ideas.

While this technique is mainly intended to adjust your thinking, if your problem involves a tangible object, it may also help to actually move the object around. Likewise, it may also help to physically move yourself to a different location, side of the room, level, or sightline.

Try these different video technique analogies:

Zoom Out: Step back to see your problem from a broader perspective. Rise to a higher altitude. Look at it in a larger context. Notice what else is involved, connected, or adjacent.

Zoom In: View your problem from a narrower perspective. Get down to the details. Take away distractions. Look at a smaller set of problems.

Pan Left: Take a look at the problem through your "left brain." That is, take a logical approach. Examine the facts and details. Think in a practical, orderly, sequential way.

Pan Right: Take a look through your "right brain." Use your imagination. Explore meaning. Consider people, values, feelings, and connections.

Change Focus and Brightness: Sharpen your focus. Increase the clarity. Examine the facts and details honestly. Shine a bright light on the problem. Then, go "fuzzy." Or dim the lights. What feeling or impression do you get?

Switch Cameras: "Cut" to a different camera. Look through the eyes of a different character. How would your customer look at the problem? How would a colleague, boss, or subordinate look at it? Where would they focus? What would an investor or public relations specialist notice?

Use Multiple Cameras: Try a "split screen" effect. Look at the problem from multiple perspectives simultaneously.

Change Camera Angles: Get underneath the problem. What are the roots? Look from the rear. What's behind it? View it from the side as well.

Adjust the Sound: Turn up the volume to intensify the problems being voiced. Then turn off the sound and just watch the visuals. Or turn up just the bass or the treble to bring out and give focus to one voice. Add some "reverb" and "hear" the echo effect. Listen carefully. What difference do these adjustments make?

Speed Up/Slow Down: Run the problem at different speeds. What do you notice if you slow it down? What stands out when you speed up?

Pause: Look at the problem from one moment in time. Try different moments. What do you notice?

Flashback/Flashforward: Look at the problem over a spectrum of time. What's happened in the past? What can you anticipate happening in the future? What influences are involved beforehand and afterward?

Apply & Evaluate: What Do You Notice?
Try some of these techniques either in the early stages of problem definition or when you are stuck. Notice:
- *What effect did changing your view have?*
- *Which techniques are most relevant to your type of problems?*
- *How else could you adjust your thinking to open up new options?*

Take Action: Now What?
When you're not making progress solving a problem, take a look from another perspective. When you change your view, you may notice different things. Check out additional ways to shift your thinking to open up new paths in the next article.

30 That's Funny! Humor As A Creativity Tool

The Challenge: You Need a Breakthrough

The Question: How Can You Open Thinking?

Consider This

"The most exciting phrase to hear in science, the one that heralds new discoveries, is not 'Eureka' but 'That's funny ... .'"
—Isaac Asimov

Try This: Laugh a Little

Using humor can be a fun and effective way to open thinking to breakthrough ideas.

Creativity and humor have a lot in common. Creativity is about doing things differently from the norm. Humor works because it takes you from the norm onto a different, unexpected path.

The Unexpected Path

Consider how jokes work. First, there is a setup line. *Why did the chicken cross the road?* It leads you to expect a certain answer. (In this case, we were probably expecting a specific reason.) Then, there is a punch line. *To get to the other side.* Not what we were expecting. (When we laugh here, we are really laughing at ourselves for overlooking the obvious.) The unexpected connection is what makes it funny.

Comic Routines
Consider methods used by comedians:
- Exaggeration, especially of something unusual, unattractive, or normally unnoticed
- Mockery, often of themselves or the human condition
- Humanization of non-human forms (e.g. a talking object or animal)
- Reversing what one would be expecting, turning things upside down
- Uncovering the obvious
- Verbalizing what may be thought, but is normally not said

All are strategies that connect a familiar topic or truth with something off our normal course of thinking.

Getting off our normal mental path opens the way to see new, creative ideas. Ironically, when we stop taking ourselves and our challenges so seriously, the solution often appears.

Think Like a Comedian
Apply techniques used in humor to open thinking to make unexpected connections:

Reverse: Sometimes underlying assumptions—either conscious or unconscious—limit our range of solutions. *What assumptions have you accepted? If you reverse them (or even remove them), what additional options appear?*

Example: *What if you switched genders or roles?* (i.e. instead of assuming men buy your product, assume your customers are women. Or instead of assuming your product is for patients, assume it is for their caregivers.)

Reverse and Exaggerate: Building on the reverse strategy, turn your challenge upside down. Go in the opposite direction. Find the worst feature. *What DON'T you want?* Then exaggerate it. This will open up new perspectives. Different challenges may appear. Truths may emerge.

Examples: *How could we lose the most money? How could we really annoy our customers? How could we make our product really ugly?*

Poke Fun: Poke fun at yourself or of "the human condition."
- *How are you, your challenge, your customers, or people in general, imperfect?*
- *What's "no win" about your situation?*
- *What is annoying?*

Example: *I can't figure out where my two-year-old picked up that colorful language.*

Humanize: Give your challenge human characteristics.
- *If your challenge could talk, what would it say?*
- *If it could feel, what emotions would it have?*

Example: *If your piano could talk, what would it say? Ooo ... that tickles!*

State the Obvious: After all, the chicken did get to the other side of the road.

Say It Out Loud: With a sense of humor, say what everyone might be thinking or fearing, but no one is saying.

Example: *I promise this breakfast meeting will be over by dinner time.*

Caution

Using elements of humor can be a good way to stimulate fresh ideas. One caution, though. What's funny to one person may be offensive in some way to another, so if using this approach in a group, take care in the choice of subject or announce "I'm joking here ... " if there's a chance of misunderstanding or sensitivity. Otherwise, you risk shutting down creativity instead of encouraging it.

Apply & Evaluate: What Do You Notice?

Next time you're looking for creative ideas, experiment with comic methods. Then consider:
- *Which techniques worked best?*
- *Where do you have to be careful not to cross the line that might offend others?*
- *When else could using humor be beneficial in your workplace?*

Take Action: Now What?

Used skillfully, humor provides many benefits in the workplace. Lighten up at the right times to combat stress, create bonds, diplomatically point to the truth, open thinking, and be memorable.

31 Creative Destruction: Break It

The Challenge: It Ain't Broke (Yet)
You've heard the familiar advice "If it ain't broke, don't fix it." Much of the time, that's smart. Your energy could be better spent other places. Not always, though.

The Question: What About Breaking It Anyway?
Consider "breaking" something on purpose if one or more of these apply:
- You anticipate change on the horizon. You can be an instigator, leader, participant in, or beneficiary of inevitable change instead of a victim.
- Improvements could produce a big benefit.
- It's almost broken or part of it is already broken. Face it.
- You want to change the world. You have a vision, resources, and energy.

> **Consider This**
>
> *"The first step in a growth policy is not to decide where and how to grow. It is to decide what to abandon. In order to grow, a business must have a systematic policy to get rid of the outgrown, the obsolete, and the unproductive."*
> —Peter Drucker

Try This: Creative Destruction
Breaking something that's "not broke" can be challenging. It takes wisdom to know when to attempt it, energy to get started, and, often, courage to overcome resistance when others are entrenched in the status quo.

When you're up to the challenge, here are a dozen "Break It" strategies to try:

Break Free
Start over from the beginning: *If you were starting up today, how would you address this issue?*

Break a Pattern
Do something to break up habitual ways of thinking, acting, or being. Forgo tried-and-true formulas. Think of yourself differently. Start in the middle and work outward. Start at the end and work backward. Skip over steps.

Break Out
Recognize the boundaries you have drawn around your challenge. Break out of the "box" entirely to see what happens. Lift off all the boundaries, qualifiers, assumptions, fears, and limits—just for now. Then see which ones, if any, are important to either reinstate or to restate a different way.

Breakdown
Look at breakdowns that have occurred. What was the cause? What would it take to fix that? What other breakdowns could occur? Look a little longer—could the breakdown lead to new opportunities?

Break In
Delve in to find the core of your challenge. What's the underlying principle, purpose, idea, or need? Explore that. Get to the guts of the matter. Then generate alternatives that address that larger issue.

For example, let's say you are working on a proposal for a new restaurant. Examples of underlying purposes related to restaurants are:
- Food
- Nutrition
- Hospitality
- Celebrations and Events

You might select one or more of those as the core to work from.

Break the Ice
Often the hardest part of any challenge is getting started. Do something to break that initial ice. Try out one idea. Take a small risk. Connect with one person. Challenge one fear.

Break Rank
Look at your challenge from the bottom up instead of the top down. How would the humblest, the smallest, the poorest, the worst, or the least likely prospect view it?

Break the Mold
Allow things to change shape. Try a different format. Change your criteria.

Break It Up
Break your challenge up into smaller challenges. Address them separately and then put them back together.

Break Off
If your challenge seems daunting, break off just a manageable piece.

Break in the Action
Give yourself a break. Stop for a while. Break away. Take a sabbatical, a vacation, or just a short mental journey somewhere else. Then return to your challenge later with fresh eyes.

Break Dance!
In breakdancing, you might work out some new "Toprock" (standing moves) and "Downrock" (footwork on the floor). You might slip in an acrobatic "Power Move" or "Freeze" and note the crowd's reaction. So, figuratively speaking, move to a different beat. Add some new tricks. Show your flair. Surprise and amaze your audience.

And one more ...

Just Break It
Just do it. Reallocate all the resources (time, energy, budget) associated with your issue to another place where they can be best used.

Apply & Evaluate: What Do You Notice?
Consider your product lines, services, processes, structure, or other scenario:
- *What might warrant "breaking"?*
- *When would it make sense for you to "break" it?*
- *Which "Break It" strategies might work best for you?*

Take Action: Now What?
Look for strategic opportunities to "break" things. Anticipate situations that are starting to change or break and take control. Look for opportunities where "breaking" the status quo could provide big benefits.

32. Innovation: It's Not Just About New Products

The Challenge: Going Beyond Product Innovation

Most people first think of innovation as the creation of new products or improvements to existing products. Product innovation can take many different forms:

- Inventions
- Improvements to existing products, such as bug fixes or added features in a software upgrade
- New or additional uses for existing products, such as cleaning uses for baking soda or creative uses for duct tape
- Extensions of existing products, such as extended warranties or training
- Repurposing of current products or materials, such as tailoring for a specific type of customer
- Creation of products from remnants
- Application of new technology to existing products

The Question: Besides Product Invention, Where Can You Innovate?

Consider This

"Everything today is ripe for reinvention and smart recombination."
—Bruce Mau, *Massive Change*

Try This: Everything's Game for Innovation
Along with inventions and product improvements, look for other ways to innovate.

Distribution and Delivery Innovation
Barnes & Noble and Amazon transformed book distribution in different ways. To transform the local bookstore experience, Barnes & Noble added cafes, comfortable seating, and other products for booklovers. Amazon not only pioneered online book sales, but now leverages their marketing and fulfillment resources to provide self-publishing services for authors and online stores for virtual retailers. Dell Computer was early in delivering custom products directly to consumers.

Potential areas for distribution and delivery innovation include:
- New types of distributors
- Distributor relationships and incentives
- Partnerships with suppliers
- Partnerships with customers
- Partnerships with non-competing businesses with similar target markets
- Distribution and delivery methods

Customer Innovation
Enterprise Rent-A-Car® took customer service a step closer by offering "we'll pick you up." E-commerce giant Wayfair started sending home decor customers to local bricks-and-mortar competitors through "Get It Near Me" pay-per-click advertising, which so far doesn't appear to be cannibalizing their online sales.[1] Instead of making you wait on hold, Apple customer service calls you back or allows you to schedule a call at a particular time.

Customer innovation can take many forms:
- Customer relationships
- Customer communication
- Customer partnerships
- Customer feedback
- Sales methods
- Customer service

Marketing Innovation
Amazon invested early in software tools that allow them to target individual customers with product suggestions based on browsing history, wish lists, previous purchases, and ratings. Uber ride service uses an innovative "surge

pricing" model to encourage additional drivers to come out during high-demand periods.

Marketing innovation can encompass a number of areas, such as:
- Marketing to new types of customers
- Customizing products
- Pricing
- Promotion methods
- Packaging
- Product bundling

New Businesses
How can you use your resources, relationships, and expertise to create new businesses? Google is using their Google Maps, Google Earth, and Street View resources and partnering with an artificial intelligence team at Stanford University to develop driverless cars. Networks such as HBO adapt their products to create regional networks such as HBO Latin America. Besides traditional dental services, my dentist now offers other services to improve your look, such as Botox.

New business opportunities may involve:
- Extended use of existing technologies
- Related services
- Partnerships
- Broadened product appeal and market
- Specialization and product niches

Production Innovation
Toyota was early in instituting "just in time" production processes, making it possible to eliminate waste and improve productivity by retrieving necessary parts as they are needed. Departing from reliance on conventional research methods, such as consumer surveys and focus groups, consulting and design firm IDEO uses "design thinking" processes, such as observation, customer road maps, prototyping, and data visualization to help their clients develop new products.

Production Innovation may entail new processes in:
- Research
- Processes
- Scheduling
- Measurement

- Quality control
- Product development

Organizational Innovation

To build the best customer service organization possible with the most committed employees, Zappos presents new employees with a radical "Offer." If recruits find during the training program that the job and company culture are not a good fit for them, Zappos will pay them a month's salary to leave. Organizations such as 3M and Google give employees a specific percentage, such as 15-20%, of their time to work on projects of their own choosing. Companies such as GE, Time Warner, and Procter & Gamble have established "reverse mentoring" programs, where younger colleagues mentor more experienced ones. These programs help the experienced partner keep up with trends and technology they might not know about, provide an opportunity for the sharing of business ideas, and increase engagement on all sides.

Organizational Innovation might involve areas as diverse as:
- Organizational structure
- Management methods
- Leadership approach
- Hiring
- Training
- Staff development
- Internal communication
- Processes
- Evaluation and metrics
- Compensation and rewards
- Work flow
- Benefits
- Job design
- Career paths

Apply & Evaluate: What Do You Notice?
Consider the full range of types of innovation:
- *In what areas could you innovate?*
- *What types of improvements could you make? What new ideas could you introduce?*
- *What can you learn from other businesses that have innovated in that area?*

Take Action: Now What?

Technological developments, globalization, and other trends are opening the way for all types of innovation. Be alert to anticipate changes that will either require you to innovate to survive or provide new opportunities to thrive.

33 Need Innovation Ideas? Listen To Your Customers

The Challenge: Creating or Improving Products and Services
Customers can be a fruitful source of ideas, particularly when they are very familiar with your product and greatly value it.

The Question: How Can You Get Ideas From Customers?
Ultimately, your success depends on customers. Let them guide you.

Consider This

"Your most unhappy customers are your greatest source of learning."
—Bill Gates

Try This: Ten Ways to Listen to Your Customer
Traditional methods of collecting customer input include:

1) **Surveys:** Ask away. Make it easy for customers to respond.

2) **Data Analysis:** Analyze customer use, competition, and trends. Dig into the numbers. New data-mining techniques take customer analysis to a new level!

3) **Customer Interviews and Focus Groups:** Longer, free-form discussions with customers may yield insights you miss with more structured surveys and data. Look for ideas to develop and test further.

When looking for input from customers, consider:
- **Customer Type:** Which will be more helpful—input from *"typical"* customers, *"special use"* customers, or *"high-use"* customers? Customers with special needs often provide ideas for targeted product extensions. High-use customers might contribute special expertise. It may be particularly important to consider the input and needs of highly-profitable customers, even if they are not "typical."
- **Volume:** From how many customers do you need input? In some cases, it will be important to have a large representative sample of customers. In other cases, thoughtful input from a smaller, targeted sample will be most helpful. For instance, a large survey or poll can give you an indication of how well things are working or help you forecast, while a small focus group of key customers can yield ideas to explore.

One of the biggest challenges in gathering input is that customers can't always envision or express what they want or need, especially if the solution doesn't already exist. As Henry Ford is said to have reflected on his development of the automobile, "If I asked people what they wanted, they would have said, 'Faster horses.'" In such cases, other methods of "listening" can be more useful:

4) **Observe:** Watch customers use your product. Do they use it in unexpected ways? What do they struggle with? What happens before and after they use it? What tweaks might help? What other opportunities appear?

5) **Catch Bugs:** Ask customers what "bugs them" about your product, along with what works well for them. It may be painful to hear the problems, but your most vocal critics are often the best source of ideas.

6) **Ask Customer-Facing Employees:** Talk with employees who deal directly with customers about their experience and frustrations. If you don't punish them as messengers, they will tell it like it is.

7) **Use User Groups:** Participate with customers in relevant forums and user groups. Notice the questions that come up most often, as well as the comments. Your most dedicated users may have already figured out workarounds for problems or product benefits and uses you never thought of. When you're thinking of making changes or improvements, consider feedback from these valuable customers.

8) **Tune In to Social Media:** Check out what others are saying about your product through social media. Look for clues where customers are "fans," as well as where they are unhappy or frustrated. People who care enough to take the time to focus on your product, even if it's negative, can provide valuable input. Consider what they are really saying or requesting.

9) **Do a Reality Check:** Compare what customers say to what they actually do with your product. (If television viewers always told the truth, public television ratings would be sky-high.)

10) **Use Your Gut:** Today's data-mining techniques have impressive capabilities and can produce amazingly detailed reports. While factual, the flood of data may either overcomplicate your search for solutions or lead you to focus on confounding variables or effects. Add a "gut check" to that fancy analysis.

Apply & Evaluate: What Do You Notice?
Consider ways your customers could be an innovation resource:
- *What aspects of your work could benefit from customer input?*
- *Which types of customer "conversations" currently yield the most useful information?*
- *What else can you do to cultivate customer relationships that will yield useful feedback?*

Take Action: Now What?
Every type of work has a customer, even if it's not a direct or external one. Who is your customer? Learn as much about them as you can. Develop customer relationships that encourage "conversation" and partnership.

34 Not Feeling Creative? Your Role In Innovation

The Challenge: On the Innovation Team, You're Not "The Idea Guy"

Perhaps you've been assigned to an innovation team or just want to develop something new yourself. In the brainstorming session, you freeze. People around you are coming up with "wild ideas." You have none. It's all you can do to obey the "don't judge" rule.

You probably have a lot more creative capacity than you currently recognize. (See *HELP! I'm Not Creative!*, p. 95.) The vast majority of us are innately creative, although we may need to rediscover and cultivate our creative talents.

If generating wildly creative ideas doesn't immediately seem like your strong suit, though, take heart. Your other specific strengths are needed in the innovation process.

The Question: How Can You Thrive in the Innovation Process?

During different stages of the innovation process, different strengths stand out. In order to make your best contribution, understand the process, as well as your own strengths.

Consider This

"Of all the things managers can do to stimulate creativity, perhaps the most efficacious is the deceptively simple task of matching people with the right assignments. Managers can match people with jobs that play to their expertise and their skills in creative thinking, and ignite intrinsic motivation."
—Teresa Amabile[1]

> *Everybody is a genius. But if you judge a fish by its ability to climb a tree, it will live its whole life believing that it is stupid.*
> —Albert Einstein

Try This: Your Innovation Role

Understand the Process
The innovation process typically involves a few distinct stages:

"Ideas and Possibilities" Stage: During this early stage, imagineers and explorers thrive. These people love change and are always looking toward the future for the next thing. They like to identify opportunities, generate ideas, and think differently.

"Translation and Implementation" Stage: During this stage, ideas are translated into systems and actions. Ideas are culled, evaluated, and tweaked. Possibilities evolve into concrete plans, processes, and actions. During this stage, adapters, activators, and negotiators shine. They are able to see both the potential of new ideas and the practical realities. They draw upon resources and put the pieces together to devise practical solutions.

"Refinement" Stage: During this stage, further refinements are made to improve ideas and processes. Details are fleshed out. Problems are identified and fixed. Practical types can use their knowledge and experience to make things work more efficiently.

These stages may continue in cycles as ideas are generated, developed, tested, and refined.

Know Yourself and Step Up Where You Are Strong
Which part of this process appealed most to you? What do you naturally notice or pay attention to that others don't?

By recognizing your own strengths, interests, and specific creative talents, you will be prepared to contribute effectively to the process.

Let Others Do What They Do Best
If you're working by yourself, understanding what's required at different stages of innovation will help you recognize when you need to shift gears. If you're working in a group, understanding the contribution of different strengths to the process will help you collaborate more effectively.

Those who shine during the "Ideas and Possibilities" stage often lose interest when it's time to think through details and practicalities. Try to give them enough space and freedom to do their best creative work without imposing too many restrictions too early.

Be ready to involve some "make it happen" types as you move into the "Translation and Implementation" stage. Let them work with a variety of stakeholders to develop systems and work through some of the early challenges. In this special role, they can serve as the bridge between ideas and activation.

As processes develop and you are moving into "Refinement," involve experts who can add detail, spot what will and won't work, and provide practical solutions. It may also be helpful to involve some of these experts and "problem-finders" early on as you test assumptions and refine your objectives. If you involve these types early, ask them to be patient and remain open so that good ideas that need some work aren't shut down before they have a chance to breathe.

Time for a Reality Check?

One of the challenges in the innovation process is balancing creativity with practicality. You may limit your potential if the creative process is shut down too soon, but practical issues must be addressed at some point. A reality check is particularly useful for two purposes:

> **Assumptions Checking:** Before you spend a lot of time fleshing out ideas and plans, check your assumptions. *Have you asked the right questions? Are you addressing the right problem? Are you aiming for an outcome that will truly be productive?* Keep asking "Why?" to direct yourself toward the most productive path.

> **Tweaking:** Test your ideas as soon as possible. See how things work in practice, look for ways to improve your results, make adjustments, and try again.

"How Could That Work?"

As you collaborate, use language that will keep thinking open and encourage solution-finding.

For instance, avoid these types of statements that tend to shut down thinking and dialogue:

- *No, that won't work.*
- *We tried that before.*
- *But ...*

Instead, use questions to open up the dialogue:
- *How could that work?*
- *What if ... ?*
- *How could we accomplish both x and y?*

Apply & Evaluate: What Do You Notice?
Next time you are involved in an innovation process, notice:
- *At which parts of the process are you naturally best?*
- *Who can you collaborate with to expand your capacity?*
- *How can your team's innovation processes be tweaked to allow for everyone's best contribution?*

Take Action: Now What?
Find your best place to contribute in the innovation process. To thrive in an environment that encourages creativity and innovation, work not only on cultivating creativity skills, but also developing your collaboration and process skills.

35 Unveil Your New Idea Strategically

The Challenge: Resistance to New Ideas
New ideas almost always meet some resistance, especially when the status quo is comfortable. Some will have an investment in keeping things the way they are. Many will simply fear the unknown. Making change often requires great commitment and energy.

The Question: How Can You Get Others to Consider New Ideas?
Innovators are often told they're crazy or worse, especially in the early stages. (Ironically, the strongest initial resistors may later be the strongest supporters—sometimes even claiming the idea as their own!)

Consider This
"If you're going to innovate ... you're going to have all these people telling you you're wrong ... It takes a lot of nerve and perseverance. You have to keep fighting the battles."
—Jeff Hawkins

Try This: Unveil Your New Idea Strategically
Prepare strategically before presenting your idea. Prepare yourself by gathering the energy and confidence to present the idea with enthusiasm. Prepare your message so others can hear it; prepare others so they will be open to it. Prepare to be spontaneous when opportunities arise to illustrate your idea and to gain support. Prepare to make adjustments if needed.

Put on Armor

When your new ideas are attacked by those invested in the status quo, fearful of the unknown, or just unable to understand the idea in the present, it may appear as a personal attack. Think of Galileo and others with new and different ideas who initially faced strong resistance. Put on protective mental armor so you don't take criticism of the idea personally. Deflect any criticism back to the idea itself. Consider adjustments and improvements to the idea. Consider a different approach in your presentation of the idea.

Connect to the Known

Connect your idea to what is already known and understood. Use an example or create an analogy. For instance, automobiles were first known as "horseless carriages." If appropriate, cite an association with a known person or organization. For instance, a testimonial from a respected person or use by a successful organization can give an idea a big boost.

Dramatize Benefits

Illustrate benefits of your idea. Demonstrate your audience's WIIFM—"What's In It For Me." Let them see it. Let them feel it. If needed, demonstrate the crisis that will occur by doing nothing.

Prepare Others

French biologist Louis Pasteur noted, "Chance favors only the prepared mind." Prepare others to be able to hear your idea. Ask them to be open. Introduce it with a frame around it to show them where to look for the benefit. Present it to them when they aren't distracted or anxious about other things. Allow time for them to chew on it.

Build Support

Begin by building support from others who have a natural interest in your idea and those who stand to benefit from it. Within that group, look for respected, influential "Opinion Leaders." Scout out credible "Early Adopters" who might be willing to try and get behind your idea.

Pre-Plan With Key Stakeholders

Anticipate additional needed support. Whose approvals or resources will be required? Who has a stake in implementing the new idea? Take account of the needs of: 1) Decision Makers, 2) Resource Providers—those who supply information, budget, tools, staff, or expertise, 3) Implementers—those who will be involved in making the idea work successfully, and 4) Gatekeepers—those who control access to these key stakeholders.

Ask for Input and Feedback

Involve these key potential supporters and stakeholders in your plan. Ask for their input. Listen to and consider their feedback. Enlist "translators" who can help make your idea more practical and understandable to others. Face concerns by asking for solutions. For instance, ask "How might we both x (achieve the benefit) and y (minimize the risk)?"

Handle Resistance

Involve resisters in resolving issues. Let refinements be their idea. Give them some credit. They are more apt to support the new idea if they have some ownership of it.

If possible, deliver bad news or controversial facts by way of a third party. For instance, cite industry statistics, media reports of competitors' plans, or an outsider's observation.

Have Patience

Give your idea time and space. If needed, let it rest and come back to it. Sometimes others need to process ideas internally. The premier of Stravinsky's revolutionary ballet *The Rite of Spring* in Paris in 1913 was met with catcalls and riots in the street. After a concert performance less than a year later, the crowd cheered and carried Stravinsky on their shoulders out into the street as a hero![1]

Minimize Risk

Most new ideas involve some level of risk. Consider how you might eliminate all or part of it. If risk can't be eliminated, consider how it could be minimized, made insignificant, or turned into an opportunity. Consider low-cost ways to try your idea out. For example, consider creating and testing a prototype with targeted customers or promoting it with a money-back guarantee.

Learn and Adjust

Not all issues can be anticipated. Take action and evaluate the results. Make adjustments and then take further action. Prepare others to expect adjustments as more information and experience are obtained. Be willing to be surprised by your learning. Many important discoveries have been made while their discoverers were looking for something else.

> *"I make more mistakes than anyone else I know and sooner or later I patent most of them."*
>
> —Thomas Edison

Be Persistent
What is clear to you may not immediately be so to others. You may need to adjust and repeat your pitch to be understood and overcome resistance.

Apply & Evaluate: What Do You Notice?
Think of a new idea you want to present:
- *How can you prepare others to be receptive?*
- *How could you minimize risk for those who try it?*
- *What obstacles can you anticipate and plan for?*

Take Action: Now What?
Congratulations. It takes courage to be an innovator.

COMMUNICATION, COLLABORATION & INFLUENCE

36 Full-Bodied Listening

The Challenge: Sometimes We Listen, But We Don't Hear
Are you a good listener? Most of us think we are, but those trying to make themselves heard may disagree.

Managers typically rate themselves higher than colleagues do in "360 degree" surveys, where a manager receives feedback from a full range of people with whom they work—superiors, peers, subordinates, and others. The biggest gap of all seems to be related to listening, particularly when it involves contrasting views and bad news.[1] Missing this information could be disastrous!

> *"The strongest human instinct is to impart information,*
> *the second strongest is to resist it."*
> –Kenneth Grahame

The Question: How Can You Improve Your "Hearing"?
Good listening goes far beyond taking in another's words with our ears.

> ### Consider This
> *"I never learn anything new when I'm the one talking."*
> —Larry King
>
> *"The most important thing in communications is to hear what isn't being said."*
> —Peter Drucker

Try This: Listen With Your Whole Body
To fully connect, listen in a variety of ways.

Listen with your ears.
- Listen for the words and the message. Listen to all of it.
- What is the speaker's tone communicating?
- What is their pace telling you?

Listen with your head.
- Does what the speaker says make sense? Is it logical and consistent?
- Nod occasionally. In fact, nod three times. This encourages the speaker to continue. (Caution: Refrain from this in cultures or cases where it may be interpreted as an "I agree" nod, instead of the intended 'I'm listening" nod.)
- Resist letting other thoughts in (such as your planned response) while you are listening.

Listen with your eyes.
- Keep good eye contact.
- What signals do you notice from the speaker's body language and facial expression?

Listen with your heart.
- What's important to the speaker?
- What is their intention?
- What do they need?
- What do you have in common?
- What do you like about what's being said?
- Connect heart-to-heart.

Listen with your gut.
- What's the message behind the message?
- Can you trust the speaker?
- What opportunities are being presented?
- What's NOT being said?

Listen with your whole body.
- Give the other your full attention.
- Lean in a little.
- Listen while you speak, too.

Apply & Evaluate: What Do You Notice?

If you're not already in a "full body" listening mode, try adding one or two elements at a time. Then notice:

- *How has your "hearing" changed?*
- *What reactions are you getting from speakers?*
- *What else could you do to listen more fully?*

Take Action: Now What?

The transformation from being a surface listener to being a deep, active listener doesn't happen overnight. Practice using good listening habits every day. It will pay off in better business results, fewer bad surprises, and improved relationships.

37) Ask, Ask, Ask: The Power Of Questions

The Challenge: Answers Are Not the Problem
Sometimes leaders think they must have all the answers. Even if you are smart and experienced, your personal knowledge and perspective may not be sufficient to come up with the best solutions for today's complex problems. On top of that, people (your teenagers, for instance, and probably your staff members, as well) often resist being told what to do or think. Things usually work better in the long-run when they come to their own answers and can do things their way.

Information is abundant these days. Google and Siri have plenty of answers. So far, though, they need to be asked. As Kevin Kelly, founding editor of *Wired* magazine, put it, "Machines are for answers; humans are for questions."[1]

Not just any question will do, however. Poorly-formed questions may skirt the core issue or take you in the wrong direction. (As they say, be careful what you ask for, because you might get it.) A leader's skillful questions can open the way to good decisions, commitment, and growth.

> *"The leader of the past was a person who knew how to tell.*
> *The leader of the future will be a person who knows how to ask."*
>
> —Peter Drucker[2]

The Question: What's the Question?
Effective questions are powerful. In a multitude of situations, the right question leads down the quickest path.

Many competencies depend on good questioning skill. For instance, good questions are the foundation for problem-solving, selling, persuading, negotiating, and influencing. Good questions help us open and direct conversations, get information, find solutions, and make good choices.

Questioning is important not only as an essential interpersonal skill, but as a tool to develop and refine our own thinking.

> **Consider This**
>
> *"You can tell whether a man is clever by his answers.*
> *You can tell whether a man is wise by his questions."*
> —Naguib Mahfouz
>
> *"I never learn anything talking. I only learn things when I ask questions."*
> —Lou Holtz
>
> *"Diagnose before you prescribe."*
> —Keith M. Eades, *The New Solution Selling*

Try This: Questions as Power Tools

Questions are like power tools. They can get the job done faster and with less effort. Pick some up and learn to use them well.

Use the Right Tool for the Job

Note the difference between two basic question structures and when each works best:

> **Open Questions:** These are broad questions used to open conversations and identify a direction to pursue further. They usually start with *What, Why,* or *How* and encourage the other person to talk. For example:
> - *What would you like to achieve?*
> - *Why are you considering a change?*
> - *How can I help?*
>
> **Closed Questions:** These are focused questions used to obtain specific information. They usually start with words like *Who, Which, When, How much,* or *Where* and can be answered in a few words. *Yes, no, blue, tomorrow, $100, Chicago, George.* For example:
> - *Do you like this?*
> - *Which color do you prefer?*
> - *When do you need it?*
> - *How much will it cost?*
> - *Where shall I send it?*
> - *Who needs to approve this?*

Notice how different types of questions are used for different purposes. For instance:

- **Diagnostic Questions** are used to obtain information, identify needs, and detect opportunities. *What are your concerns? What would be ideal? What would it take?*
- **Provocative Questions** challenge and stimulate thinking. *What's likely to happen if you do nothing? To what extent is x a problem for you? If there were a way to do y, would you be interested?*
- **Clarifying and Confirming Questions** ensure understanding. *If I understand you correctly, you're looking for x—is that right? What exactly do you mean by "y"?*

"There's No Such Thing as a Dumb Question," Right?
If a question occurs to you, it's probably not dumb. It may not be one that's smart to share, though. Watch out for these three kinds of question traps:

Inappropriate Questions: Some questions may technically be good ones, but inappropriate in some way:

- **Bad timing:** It's too early, too late, or too sensitive a time to ask.
- **Wrong person:** You're wasting energy asking someone who can't respond or act.
- **Wrong role:** You're not the right person to ask that question. For instance, it's too personal to ask within a business relationship or it's not your place to ask.
- **Manipulation:** The question undermines trust by attempting to trap someone with accusatory, leading, or loaded language.

Ineffective Questions: At certain times or under certain circumstances, asking questions may diminish your effectiveness:

- **Should have done your homework:** Some questions could reveal your lack of preparation.
- **Don't advertise your weaknesses:** Certain questions might expose your shortcomings at inopportune times.
- **No need to ask:** Sometimes it's wise and necessary to ask permission. When it's not, asking may slow you down, conjure up new problems, and make you appear less competent.
- **Conversation Closers:** Phrasing that suggests superiority, threat, or blame may put the other person on the defensive or cause them to clam up.

- **"Upspeak":** When you intend to make a statement, but your voice rises at the end as if you are asking a question, you appear less confident.
- **Misfits:** Some questions haven't been thought through or aren't phrased to get the desired response. (For example, asking a closed question that gets a one-word response, instead of an open one that would be more likely to uncover richer information.)

Irrelevant Questions: Surface questions don't get to the root issue; peripheral questions take up time while taking you off course.

Be question-savvy. Prepare in advance. Use the questions appropriate for the occasion. Phrase them skillfully.

Three Power Questions
Three simple, but extremely powerful questions are:

Oh? Information is power. Keep the other person talking with a simple indication of interest and curiosity. *Mmmm. Tell me more. What else? Who else? How else?*

Why? Get to the root of the issue with a simple *"Why?"* Keep asking until you get there. To avoid sounding like a three-year-old, vary your subsequent whys slightly—*What do you hope to accomplish? What's your interest?*

How Might We ... ? Generate solutions by directing thought to your desired outcomes. *How might we accomplish both x and y?*

Watch Your Delivery
Assuming your purpose is to get information or devise solutions, ask your questions in a way that puts the other person at ease and encourages their thoughtful response. Use open body-language and a friendly tone. Frame your question so it doesn't put them on the defensive. Be conversational; don't bombard the other person; vary your language and questions. Pause and give them a chance to think and respond. Show that you're listening.

20 Favorite Questions for Results
Did you ever play the game "20 Questions"? Here are some favorite questions for a variety of purposes and occasions.
   1) Productivity: *What's the best use of my time, energy, and attention right now?*
   2) Learning: *What's the principle?*
   3) Business Strategy: *Who is our customer?*

4) Creativity: *What are we assuming? What could be changed?*
5) Solution-Finding: *What if ... ?*
6) Selling: *Who will be involved in making this decision? ... Who else?*
7) Persuading: *What criteria will you use to decide?*
8) Negotiating: *What's most important to you here?*
9) Leadership: *Why should anyone follow you?*
10) Personal Decisions: *What difference will it make in ... (50 years, 10 years, a year, a month, 10 minutes)?*
11) Leadership Decisions: *Which choice provides the greatest good for the greatest number?*
12) Teams: *What are our three most important team goals in order of priority?* (*... and if there are times when they are in conflict with individual goals, how will we handle that?*)
13) Performance Coaching: *What have you tried? What else could you try? What will you do?*
14) Responding to Feedback: *What specific suggestions do you have on how I can improve? What would that look like?*
15) Work-Life Balance: *How do you define "success"?*
16) Interviewing for a Job: *In this position, what sets top performers apart from the rest?*
17) Hiring: *If I called your previous bosses (colleagues, customers, or anyone else you might actually call for a reference), what would they tell me about your ... (work ethic, performance, teamwork, etc.)?*
18) Networking: *What are you working on?*
19) Failure and Adversity: *What can I learn from this?*
20) Finally: *When is enough enough?*

Apply & Evaluate: What Do You Notice?

As you go about your work and life this week, practice your questioning skills. Consider:
- *When can you get farther by asking, rather than telling?*
- *Which questions give you the best results?*
- *When is it best to hold your questions?*

Take Action: Now What?

Keep a collection of your own favorite questions and keep asking!

P.S. When you ask, don't forget to listen to the answers.

38) Showing Up As Your Best: The Impact Of Nonverbal Communication

The Challenge: Making a Good Impression and Commanding Attention

As a leader of any kind, you'll be required to "show up" in front of others in a compelling, credible, and confident way, whether that involves speaking in front of a large group, directing a small group meeting, or communicating one-on-one.

The Question: How Can You Show Up as Your Best?

> **Consider This**
>
> *"You are the message."*
> —Roger Ailes

Try This: Don't Neglect the All-Important 55%

First Impressions Count!
Social psychologists find that most people form initial impressions of each other within 5–20 seconds. This "first impression" is typically a "gut" reaction to nonverbal factors such as:
- Posture
- Body language
- Facial expression
- Gestures
- Eye contact
- Personal space
- Dress and appearance
- Tone of voice

The Impact of Nonverbal Communication: 55%

Even after this initial impression, these nonverbal factors play a significant role in personal effectiveness. According to UCLA Professor of Psychology Dr. Albert Mehrabian's famous study of "Silent Messages," tone of voice and body language play a significant role in how much we like and believe a speaker. He found that, **when talking about feelings or attitudes, words alone account for only 7% of the speaker's likability, while tone of voice accounts for 38% and body language 55%.** Additionally, he found that if these elements aren't congruent, we tend to trust the nonverbal elements rather than the literal words.[1] Most of the time, the nonverbal message is expressed and interpreted subconsciously.

Interpretation of nonverbal communication can vary according to culture. The following suggestions are made for North Americans.

Posture: Posture particularly conveys confidence, energy, and interest. It reflects a combination of mental state and physical habit. Explore how posture changes based on your mental state. For example, note how your posture might change if you were feeling very proud versus feeling depressed. Then experiment with the reverse; explore how your mental state changes when you change your posture. Does a "power pose" make you feel more confident?

Generally, the most effective posture, both for speaking and for creating a strong impression, is straight with shoulders slightly back, but slightly relaxed. This creates an impression of confidence and credibility, while also allowing you to breathe deeply and speak with a strong, lower-pitched voice.

Body Language: Intentional or unintentional body movements, poses, gestures, and facial expressions may suggest mental states such as defensiveness, aggression, or nervousness; or suggest possible dishonesty, disinterest, or weakness. Notice your reaction to someone with:
- Slumped shoulders
- Fingers on lips
- Closed fists
- Arms folded over chest
- A habit of fiddling nervously with accessories or clothing
- A limp handshake

According to body language experts, these all send signals that detract from one's power and message. For instance, closed fists or arms folded over the chest convey nervousness or defensiveness. Slumped shoulders and limp handshakes convey weakness. Fingers on your lips suggest you might be holding something back. Fiddling signals boredom.

Adopt more effective body language:
- Alert posture with head held high
- Standing straight when speaking; leaning forward slightly when listening
- Open body stance without crossed legs, feet, or arms
- Feet pointing where you want to go
- Arms slightly in front of you around waist level with elbows bent or relaxed at your sides
- Palms up to convey openness; palms open toward yourself to draw others to your ideas; palms down to convey authority
- Pleasant facial expression—a genuine smile, if appropriate
- Firm, but not crushing, handshake with good eye contact
- Hand offered with your palm in vertical position to convey equality

Some body language experts suggest subtly mirroring the other person's body language.

Eye Contact: Eye contact can be used to:
- Establish or determine a level of trust.
- Check for understanding.
- Pick up nonverbal signals.

Good eye contact is needed to establish credibility. Eye contact that is too intense, however, can create distrust or discomfort. A suggested guideline is to maintain eye contact approximately 75% of the time while talking and listening.

Personal Space: Some individuals have a strong reaction to what they perceive as an invasion of their "personal space." While acceptable personal space can vary significantly by culture and individual, cultural anthropologist Edward T. Hall, known for his research on the effect of personal space in interpersonal communication, suggests these general guidelines for personal space:
- Intimate Distance: 6–18 inches
- Personal Distance: 1.5–4 feet
- Social Distance (appropriate for business interactions): 4–12 feet
- Public Distance (used for public speaking): 12 feet or more[2]

Dress and Appearance: Dress and appearance affect perception of credibility, competence, and fit. Appropriate dress depends both on the culture and the specific situation. In general:
- Think "polished and professional."
- When in doubt, dress up.

- For interviews, dress for the position 1–2 levels above the one for which you are interviewing.
- Avoid clothes or accessories that will distract from you and your message.
- Remember that accessories, such as a good briefcase or bag, portfolio, or writing pad and pen, are an important part of your appearance.

Vocal Power: Your voice also plays a vital role in how you and your message are received. To speak more powerfully using the lower part of your vocal range, stand tall, breathe deeply, and stay relaxed through your shoulder, neck, and throat areas. Vary your tone, volume, and pace to dramatize your message. Pause to let your message sink in.

Last Impressions Count, Too
Along with our first contact with someone, we tend to remember our most recent contact. Conclude your communication effectively, both verbally and nonverbally, whether it's with a handshake, a smile, or a confident walk.

Apply & Evaluate: What Do You Notice?
Observe effective leaders and pay attention to their nonverbal communication. (You might even turn down the audio while watching them on video.) Notice their posture and gestures:
- *How does their "look" affect your impression of them?*
- *How do they command attention? What type of posture and gestures are effective?*
- *What can you learn from them as you hone your presentation style?*

Take Action: Now What?
When you prepare to give a talk, run a meeting, or just participate in a conversation, keep in mind the impact of nonverbal communication. Practice delivering important messages in front of a mirror, or record and then watch yourself, paying attention to your posture, gestures, eye contact, and facial expression. Make an effort to create a strong first and last impression.

39) May I Have Your Attention, Please?

The Challenge: Your Audience's Mental Noise
Your listeners' heads and schedules may be full even before they consider listening to you. Attention spans have become shorter and multitasking more prevalent. Inside your listener's head it might sound something like this:
- "Hmm—I just got a new text. I wonder who it's from?"
- "I wonder what's going on ... (in the other room, on the other channel, back home ...)"
- "My boss needs ... "
- "My kids need ... "
- "I need ... "
- "What time's lunch?"
- zzzzzzzzz ...

The Question: How Can You Get Your Audience's Attention?
With all that going on, why should they listen to you?

> **Consider This**
>
> *"The more personal the context, the greater the interest."*
> —Frank Luntz, *Words That Work*
>
> *"The key to being fully heard is to listen to your audience even while you are speaking to them."*
> —Lee Glickstein, *Be Heard Now*
>
> *"Be sincere. Be brief. Be seated."*
> —Franklin D. Roosevelt

Try This: Get Inside Your Listeners' Heads
Put yourself in your listeners' shoes. Better yet, get inside their heads.

What Else is Vying for Their Attention?
Before you even approach your audience, consider what else may be vying for their attention. Good timing can make a big difference in receptivity. If you have some flexibility, consider the best time to approach them. Most of us are not good listeners when we are hungry, tired, physically uncomfortable, angry, emotional, in crisis, or under pressure to meet a big deadline.

Why Should They Listen?
Whether consciously or unconsciously, your listeners are sizing up the situation and deciding whether they are going to open up their headspace to take you in or just not bother.

Here's what they want to know:
- *Is this relevant to me?*
- *Why should I listen?*
- *(And they still probably really want to know: When is lunch?)*

Did you see anything in that list about you? Nope. They're probably not dying to know about your product or opinion. To get their attention, the message has to be about THEM.

Organize Your Message From Their Point of View.
Know your audience. Pretend you are them. If you were your listener, what would you want to know? What would already be on your mind? How would you want to feel?

Address their "WIIFM"—What's In It For Me. Frame your message according to what's important and beneficial to them.

How would your audience members identify themselves? Use the language they would use to describe themselves and the language they would use to talk about their problems.

Who Are You, Anyway?
Now if, and only if, they decide there's something worth their time, they will also want to know two things about you:
1) *Do you care about them? (Can they trust that you understand them and have their best interests at heart?)* AND
2) *Do you know what you're talking about?*

Make an effort to connect personally first. Be human and likable. Do your homework and then show you care by tailoring your message to their concerns. Speak their language. Choose words and questions that create rapport and open thinking. Avoid contentious language. Remember that words alone account for only 7% of a speaker's likability, while tone of voice accounts for 38% and body language 55%[1]. Sprinkle in a dash of background information that shows you are qualified to address your topic.

Keep Them Awake
If you suspect your audience's attention is drifting, be ready to do something to recapture it. For instance:
- Say or show something surprising. Make a bold statement, use a dramatic statistic, or show a dramatic image.
- Move toward them.
- Use your voice expressively. Avoid speaking in a monotone. Change your volume; speak up or whisper. Vary the pace. Use pauses to create space.
- Change height. Stand up or get down to their eye level.
- Use humor.
- Hand them something.

Watch, Listen, and Adapt
Watch for nonverbal cues. Women tend to show what they're thinking more through facial expression, while men tend to reveal it through body language.[2] If the signs are receptive, keep going. Otherwise, make some adjustments and keep watching the response.

Next time you're trying to get a message across, get inside your listener's head first. They'll be grateful.

Apply & Evaluate: What Do You Notice?
When you have a message to deliver, first ask yourself:
- *What does your audience care about?*
- *Why should they listen to your message?*
- *How can you break through their mental noise?*

Take Action: Now What?
Practice delivering your messages—whether written or verbal, formal or informal—from your listeners' point of view.

40) Make Your Message Memorable

The Challenge: Information Overload
Audiences today are often distracted, overloaded with information, and easily bored. In the end, your audience members will likely take away just a few key points from your presentation, along with a feeling about you.

The Question: What Do You Want Them to Remember?

> **Consider This**
>
> *"It's not what you say, it's what they hear."*
> —Frank Luntz
>
> *"I've learned that people will forget what you said, people will forget what you did, but people will never forget how you made them feel."*
> —Maya Angelou

Try This: Make Your Message Memorable
Find out as much as you can about your audience and then organize your message around their needs and interests. Clearly define your desired outcome. Then, aim for it with a relevant, captivating, and concise message.

Design Your Message for Impact
Use this seven-question process to formulate a memorable message:

1) **What's most important to your audience?** Keep that in mind and frame your message to relate to their interests. They're more apt to remember information they find truly interesting and relevant.

2) **If they only remembered <u>one</u> thing as a result of your talk, what would you want that to be?** Plan to get that across early and often, clearly and consistently. Consider making it into a short slogan. Three words are ideal.

3) **How do you want them to <u>feel</u> as a result of your talk?** Feelings are often remembered long after the facts are forgotten and issues pass. As you choose how you will frame your message and the language you will use, consider the impact on feelings.

4) **What do you want your listeners to <u>do</u> as a result of your talk?** Plant seeds at the beginning. Water them as you go. Bring in the harvest at the end by asking your audience to act.

5) **If the audience took away <u>three</u> things from your talk, what would you want them to be?** For a longer talk, organize your material around up to three major points. Decide on the most effective order to present them. State, dramatize, provide evidence for, and summarize each; then bring them all together at the end.

6) **What is different or urgent this time?** What makes your point or "ask" especially compelling at this time?

7) **What other major concerns does the audience have?** Be sensitive and prepared to address them if they come up.

Help Them Remember

To counter today's constant information deluge, employ these seven techniques to help listeners remember your message:

1) **Address a specific problem your listener cares about solving.**

2) **Use multiple tactics to illustrate or support your "takeaway" points.** For example:
    - Tell a story that makes the point. Use familiar characters and relevant situations.
    - Show evidence to support your point. Surprising statistics are good; physical evidence is better.
    - Use visuals to reinforce your message. As the saying goes, "A picture is worth a thousand words."
    - Reinforce your point by repeating it throughout your presentation.

3) **Use contrast to set your message apart.** Show before and after. Show best case versus worst case. Use white space. Use silence.

4) **Employ memorable language.** For example:
    - Draw a mental picture with specific vivid language. Remember "onomatopoeia" from English class? Use a word that sounds like its meaning, such as *bang, slither* or *flutter*.
    - Use linguistic devices. You might think it sounds cheesy, but devices such as alliteration, repetition of a letter or sound in adjacent words (e.g. *Listen Loudly*), or rhyming (*"Funny is Money"*) can be very "catchy."
    - Devise an acronym, such as the familiar advice to presenters: KISS, Keep It Simple, Stupid.

5) **If your topic is new or complex, make it easier to understand and remember by connecting it with something your listener already knows.** For instance, use an analogy of something familiar. (*You know how you've upgraded your computer software? Have you upgraded your own mental tools?*)

6) **Involve the audience.** Ask questions. Take a poll. Include a quiz or exercise. Let them finish your sentence. Do something together. Stop and check in to see how they're doing. Encourage them to apply the information to their specific situation. Give them a worksheet to fill in.

7) **Position yourself memorably.** We tend to remember what comes first and what comes last. If you're in a lineup of several speakers, aim to go first or last. We also tend to remember what is different, so position yourself in some unique way to stand out.

Apply & Evaluate: What Do You Notice?
As you prepare to deliver an important message, pinpoint:
- *What one thing do you want your audience to remember?*
- *How do you want them to feel as a result of your talk?*
- *What do you want them to do as a result of your talk?*

Take Action: Now What?
After you give a presentation, collect feedback to determine what your audience actually took away from it. Then make adjustments if needed to boost the impact of upcoming presentations.

41. Prepare Your Audience

The Challenge: Getting Your Audience On Your Page
When you start a conversation or presentation, your audience is thinking about all sorts of other things. Even as they begin to focus on your topic, they may be coming with very different interests, backgrounds, opinions, and expectations related to your message.

The Question: How Can You Quickly Prepare Your Audience to Hear Your Message?
As you begin, capture your audience's attention and guide them to the path on which you want them to travel. If it's a controversial topic, give them a reason to be open. If it's a broad topic, point them to the aspect on which you want them to focus.

Consider This
"People only see what they are prepared to see."
—Ralph Waldo Emerson

Try This: "Frame" Your Message to Direct Your Audience's Attention
Have you ever visited a frame shop and experimented with different frames? If so, you probably noticed that the frames you chose made a big difference in how your artwork appeared. For instance, a colored frame or mat around a picture might make specific elements "pop." A thick frame gives a much different feel than a thin one. Changing out a wood frame for a metal one alters the mood. A stylistic frame might transport you back to a different era. A different finish or texture adds flavor.

The choice of physical frame can make a difference in what you notice, what stands out, and how you feel when viewing a piece of art.

Frame

Your

Message

Similarly, you can "frame" your message to set a tone and direct your audience's focus. Take a moment to set up your conversations to ensure connection and show others where you want them to "look."

When to Frame
Framing provides context for a conversation or meeting in several ways. When you are giving a speech, making a presentation, bringing up a point in a

meeting, pitching an idea to a colleague, or making a request, a "frame" can be used to:
- Set the tone.
- Warm up your audience.
- Position your topic.
- Get everyone "on the same page."
- Communicate intent.
- Draw boundaries around the discussion.
- Indicate emphasis.
- Convey assumptions.
- Establish yourself as a leader.
- Provide context when you shift to a new topic.

Choosing Your Frame

If you visit a master framer, before showing you frames, they might ask:
- *What do you want to showcase?*
- *What mood do you want to create?*
- *What style fits the art and the place it will hang?*

Along those same lines, as you create a frame for your message, consider these questions:
- *What's the agenda today?*
- *What's the big overarching idea, theme, or purpose you want your audience to see?*
- *What's the intended outcome? What do you want them to understand, feel, or do at the end of the conversation?*
- *What do they need to know to be able to start at the same point you are?*
- *Whom or what do you need to acknowledge?*

Framing Tools: Directing Focus

A framer uses different elements to create the desired "look"—a variety of woods or materials, textures, colors, types of glass, and background mats.

In framing your message, tools you can work with to position your message include:

Title: The title of your talk or agenda item guides your audience's expectations. Connect to your audience and their interests by including words or phrases in the title that make them think, *Oh, that's me you're talking about. That's what I want to hear about. That's the need I have. That's the benefit I want.*

Story or Humor: When you open with a short story or joke, the "moral of the story" or "punch line" orients the listener to your theme. Choose and describe characters and the situation in a way that the audience can see themselves in your tale.

Language: Your specific choice of words can add color and mood. Choose words that will elicit the feelings you want to create.

Images: Save your words. Show an image to dramatize a need you are going to address.

Links: Link your message to someone or something with whom or which you want it associated.

Analogy: If you're introducing an unfamiliar concept, use an analogy to connect it to something your audience already knows. For instance, relate it to some aspect of weather, cooking, or sports.

Bring It Back
Having set up your topic to show where you want the audience to focus, you can then refer to that as you make your points and then again as you wrap up at the end.

Apply & Evaluate: What Do You Notice?
Next time you are preparing for a presentation or important meeting, try out a few "frames" on your message. Consider:
- *How can I quickly capture my audience's interest?*
- *On what aspect of my message do I want them to focus?*
- *What outcome am I aiming for?*

Take Action: Now What?
Practice ways to quickly orient your listener. Skill in framing your messages can improve your efficiency, connection, and impact, not only in professional situations, but in everyday conversations.

42 In A World Of Too-Much-Information, Less Is More

The Challenge: The Incredible Shrinking Attention Span
We're Bombarded By Messages
While you are reading this sentence, information is exponentially increasing. According to internetlivestats.com, more than 7,000 messages are tweeted, 120,000 YouTube videos are viewed, and 2.4 million emails are sent EVERY SECOND!

This Year's Lifetime of Information
Information experts point out that we are now exposed to more new information in one year than the average person born in 1900 was in an entire lifetime. The amount continues to increase every year.

Smaller Sound Bites
During the last 50 years, short phrases have increasingly been used in media to capture the essence of stories. The length of the average "sound bite" in American presidential news coverage has declined steadily—from 42 seconds in 1968 to 9.8 seconds in 1988 to 7.3 seconds in 2000, according to the Center for Media and Public Affairs.[1] While this limited type of message may be incomplete or even misleading, we've become accustomed to hearing these short informational bursts.

Texting While Talking?
With the proliferation of websites, social media, and smartphones, audiences are increasingly likely to be splitting their attention between multiple information sources and messages.

As Kevin Kelley, cofounder of *Wired* magazine put it, *"The only factor becoming scarce in a world of abundance is human attention."*[2]

The Question: How Can You Break Through the Communication Clutter?

With all of this informational noise, it's becoming more difficult to be "heard" and remembered.

> **Consider This**
>
> *"Less is more."*
> –Ludwig Mies Van der Rohe

Try This: Lasering

Use a "lasering" technique to deliver important messages. Just as a laser emits a focused beam of light, concentrate your message into a few concise, powerful words for maximum impact.

Just. Three. Words.

Boil your point down to three words (unless you can boil it down to just one!) Three is a magic number. Attention starts to dissipate after that.

Say your three words. Pause. Check to see if it connected with your audience. If you've been able to tap their attention, you may then have the opportunity to expand your message. Try 10-12 more words, about the length of today's average "soundbite." Check again and expand from there, if appropriate.

Focus On Them

Choose specific words to connect with your listener. For instance, use "you," their name, something they value, or your message's benefit to them. Even better, after you have their attention, engage them with a question or involve them in some other way.

Bright, Shiny Objects

Use visuals or visual language to dramatize your point. Capture the listener's interest by raising provocative questions. Instead of vague terms (such as "great," "nice," or "interesting") choose specific, colorful language (such as "lucrative," "polished," or "gripping").

Lather. Rinse. Repeat.
Help your listener remember your point by sprinkling your three magic words throughout your conversation or follow-up communication. You don't want to be tiresome—just memorable.

Use With Care
Of course, you won't want to "laser" all the time. In some situations, it might be annoying, limiting, or even irresponsible. Avoid lasering where greater depth and breadth of information is required. In such cases, it can still be used to summarize the essence of a longer message.

Apply & Evaluate: What Do You Notice?
Try this "lasering" technique when you need to break through the clutter. Then assess:
- *Were you heard?*
- *Were you effective?*
- *What was the result?*

Take Action: Now What?
Think of situations where lasering would be effective—for instance, as a conversation-opener, as an intriguing answer, to bring a long-winded discussion to closure, in email subject lines, or perhaps even to get through to a disinterested teenager.

Add this technique to your communication toolkit and pull it out when the occasion calls for it.

43 Watch Your Language!

The Challenge: Drawing In and Engaging Listeners

The Question: How Can You Choose Words to Set the Right Tone?

Consider This

"Language is the dress of thought."
—Samuel Johnson

"Think like a wise man, but communicate in the language of the people."
—William Butler Yeats

"You may choose your words like a connoisseur,
And polish it up with art,
But the word that sways, and stirs, and stays,
Is the word that comes from the heart."
—Ella Wheeler Wilcox

"Drawing on my fine command of the English language, I said nothing."
—Robert Benchley

Try This: Purposefully Use the Words They Long to Hear

Early in my career, I had an opportunity to tag along with an industry association group on a couple of lobbying trips. As the most junior person on the trip, I didn't have a speaking role, but the opportunity to watch and listen to the professional politicians was fascinating.

Noncommittal Language

I found myself collecting phrases they used to make their audience feel good without really committing to anything. In response to our pitches, they said they'd:

keep it in mind
take it into consideration
look into
review
note
explore
assess
investigate

and led us to believe that agreement was:
possible
likely
conceivable
an option

That is, ...
if
maybe
perhaps

Was anybody really buying this???

Buying Words

Then, as a marketer, mentors shared lists of persuasive words that drive potential customers to buy or take action.

The top word was *You*, followed by perennial favorites such as *free, money, save, new, results, health, easy, safe, love, discovery, proven, guarantee,* and *sale*.

Being more of a "numbers person," I had never given much thought to the effect certain words could have. I was hooked.

Language of Accountability and Results

As I moved up the corporate ladder, I found that higher-ups responded to certain words.

They were hungry to hear **Results Words**, such as *outcome, improvement, and profit*. Their ears would perk up anticipating *proposals, recommendations,* and *solutions*. They loved **Accountability Words**, such as *commitment, performance, completion, responsibility, criteria, requirements, deliverables,* and *consequences*.

The finance guys responded to **Money Words**, like *profitability, revenue, margins, savings, and cost-effective*. In planning, they'd use **Strategy Words**, such as *anticipate, evaluate, analyze, strategize, and prioritize* leading to **Action Words** like *initiate, decide, launch, produce, expedite, and schedule*.

If they'd read the latest business bestsellers, they'd sprinkle in **Business Book Words**, such as *excellence, sustainable, streamline, and innovate*.

When they smelled potential danger, they'd throw around **CorporateSpeak**, such as:

- *Challenges (big problems)*
- *Opportunities (big challenges)*
- *Feasible (it's possible, but we don't want to)*
- *Reevaluation (we goofed the first time around; now we have to fix it)*
- *Transition (we're having a few more problems post-reevaluation)*

A few got in legal trouble when it was discovered that they had used certain words in communication related to competitors: *dominate, eliminate,* and *prevent*.

Language of Cooperation and Rapport

Later, in various leadership roles and as a negotiator, I found myself in situations where I needed to get cooperation without having formal authority or power. I observed that certain words would make people nervous and shut down the conversation—*No, never, won't, can't,* and *but*—and some were likely to hit a nerve—*mistake, refuse, damage, lie, ridiculous, crazy, stupid,* and *wrong*.

Watching skilled negotiators, I noticed they would **Set a Tone** with words that hinted at a reasonable approach, such as *welcome, goodwill, common goals, productive, purpose, relationship, trust, willing,* and *consider*.

They'd then **Convey Inclusion** with words such as *we, us, our, team, together, listen, include, invite, mutual, partnership,* and *interest*. They'd **Get Input** by asking for your *perspective, opinion, advice,* or *reaction*. They might even **Share Credit** with words such as *appreciate, contribution, resource, together, acknowledge,* and *thanks*.

To show they would **Consider Different Viewpoints**, they'd *listen, hear, confer, huddle, dialogue, discuss,* and *explore* looking for *facts, information,* and *understanding*. To **Demonstrate Cooperation**, they'd *collaborate, coordinate, accommodate, offer, consider, work with, agree, respond,* and *support*. They'd say Yes as many times and ways as possible. Then, they'd work to **Create Solutions** with words such as *recommend, suggest, work out,* and *resolve*.

Language of Opportunity and Vision

As an aspiring entrepreneur and innovator, I fervently studied creativity research and methods. In doing so, I identified language that opens thinking to new ideas.

Words such as *explore, potential, create, synergy, partner,* and *transform* raise interest and suggest collaboration. In an idea generation session, questions such as *"What if?", "Why?",* and *"How can we?"* open the flow. *Curious, investigate, imagine, ideal,* and *optimal* inspire dialogue, while *feasible, alternatives, possibility,* and *Yes!* keep it *moving forward.*

Apply & Evaluate: What Do You Notice?

Listen to effective leaders of all types, taking note of language they use to unify, inspire, and influence. Pay attention to advertising copy. Note subject lines that raise your interest or curiosity enough to get you to open email right away. Notice:

- *When you are the audience, to which words do you respond well? Which words "turn you off"?*

Then, next time you make a pitch or facilitate a conversation, experiment with purposeful language. Consider:

- *How might choice of words make a difference in that conversation?*
- *Which words will serve your purpose? Which words are likely to "turn off" your audience?*

Take Action: Now What?

Continue to listen for and learn to use different types of language to purposefully set the tone you want for your conversation. Also consider ways you can work the language your listener uses into your communication, while avoiding using your own jargon.

44 Got Stage Fright?

The Challenge: Being Nervous In Front of a Crowd
If you get nervous when you are called upon to speak or perform in public, you have a lot of company. Fear of public speaking is Americans' biggest phobia.[1] Even experienced presenters and performers may struggle with pre-performance jitters.

The Question: How Can You Best Prepare to Face an Audience?
Whether you're preparing to give a speech, lead a large meeting, perform as a musician, or take part in any other type of presentation, there are several steps you can take to handle nervousness so your message can shine through.

Consider This

"There are only two types of speakers in the world: 1) The nervous and 2) Liars."
—Mark Twain

Try This: Think Like an Actor
Get in a performance mindset as actors do.

Prepare to Go "On Stage"
Build confidence through solid preparation. Consider ten ways actors prepare to go on stage and how their routines might apply to your "performance."

- ★ **Study your "Role."** A saying among teachers and performers that I've found to be true is "If you can't do it in practice, you won't do it in performance." Nothing substitutes for knowing your stuff.
- ★ **Understand your "Motivation."** Be clear on your purpose.
- ★ **Rehearse key "Lines."** Practice important parts until they flow smoothly and effortlessly.

- ★ **Visualize a successful "Performance."** Picture in your mind how you want your performance to go. Anticipate various scenarios that could occur and how you will handle them.
- ★ **Know the "Stage," the "Stagehands," the other "Actors," and the "Play."** Become familiar with the venue in which you'll be working. Get to know your collaborators. Know not just your own part, but how it fits into the overall context.
- ★ **Choose an appropriate "Costume."** Dress in something fitting for your role, flattering, and comfortable to work in. Once you put it on, you don't want to have to worry about it. If you will be working under hot lights or tend to perspire heavily, dress accordingly.
- ★ **Consult "Make Up" to highlight your best features and downplay flaws.** Have an experienced and objective third party check both your appearance and presentation visuals, provide feedback, and help you make adjustments to look your best.
- ★ **Select fitting "Props."** Bring materials you'll need to support your "Act." Sometimes it helps to have something to hold onto; don't fiddle with it, though. Test tech tools, microphones, and remotes in advance. Have water and a tissue handy.
- ★ **Be ready to make your "Entrance" on cue.** Arrive early so nothing keeps you from being "in your place."
- ★ **"Get in Character" and stay there.** People will be watching you, not only while you're saying your own lines, but all the time. Make sure you are conveying the character you want to portray, not only in your official words or performance, but also in your "look" and informal interactions with others.

Got Stage Fright?

Does your nervousness show up in physical symptoms, such as a racing pulse, pounding heart, or stomach "butterflies"? If so, here are a few tips to deal with them:

- **Understand "Fight or Flight" syndrome:** The nerves you may be feeling are not a personal flaw. Our natural wiring sets us up to be on high alert during potentially dangerous times. In an earlier era, the extra adrenaline you are feeling would have allowed you to fight or flee from dangerous predators.
- **Release nervous energy:** If you're out of sight "backstage," work your big muscles. Move around. Stretch. Do a few wall push-ups. Even "punch it out." If you are sitting in a meeting or are somewhere visible, discreetly tense and release your fists.

- **Breathe:** Take several deep breaths. This will help calm both mind and body.
- **Go back to your purpose:** Your purpose is bigger than this resistance that tries to hold you back, right?
- **A little mental shift can make a big difference:** Even some of the most experienced performers and presenters feel nervous. In some ways it's a good sign—a sign of caring about what you are about to deliver to others. Shift your mental focus away from self, from "being nervous" (focusing on how *you* feel) to "being excited" (focusing on what you can do for *others*).
- **Develop your own pre-performance ritual:** Work out your best pre-performance way of staying calm and focused, whether that is exercise, breathing, meditation, or a little warm-up routine.

Make Your Entrance

Getting off to a good start is crucial. Make a confident entrance. Don't rush. Before you do anything else, breathe and use eye contact to connect with the audience. Give yourself a moment to plant your feet and get centered. If you are able to rehearse in advance, give special attention to your entrance and the beginning of your presentation or performance. Practice it until it flows easily.

Being "On Stage"

While you are performing or presenting, keep calm, keep alert, and keep focused. Stay in the moment. Shut out distractions and don't let your thoughts wander. Worry about other things later.

Watch for Cues

Listen intently during meetings and watch for cues. Read the body language of the other participants. Do they seem engaged? When others make comments or ask questions, listen not only to their words, but to the tone and for the intent. Be cognizant of the feeling in the room and adjust as needed.

Still Nervous?

It probably doesn't show. Really. Breathe deeply. Concentrate on your purpose and message.

Made a Mistake?

It happens all the time. If it's important to correct yourself, do. Most of the time, however, if you keep going, it's unlikely many will ever know or remember your blip. If you start strong, connect well with your audience, and finish strong, they will usually walk away with a good feeling and remembrance of 1-3 points.

The Big Finish
People tend to remember their first impression and their most recent impression. Plan an effective ending and exit, including a bit of memorable content, good eye contact, a genuine smile, and a confident walk.

One More Thing
Remember that you're not "offstage" until you're completely out of sight—of everyone. Keep your head up and keep a smile on your face. Even when you're off the official stage, you are "on" with "stagehands" or organizers. When you leave "backstage" you are likely to be "on" with audience members and others. Even after you've left the building, you may still be in sight. When you get behind your door at home, you can totally relax (unless you are a parent, in which case, take another deep breath—the next act begins)!

Apply & Evaluate: What Do You Notice?
Becoming more confident and comfortable speaking or performing involves a combination of preparation, method, mindset, and experience. Before your next "performance," consider:
- *How can you best prepare your content?*
- *How can you prepare mentally?*
- *What other practical steps can you take to prepare?*

Take Action: Now What?
Take every good opportunity you can to speak, perform, or lead a meeting. As with most skills, being in front of others gets easier with practice and experience.

45 How To Get People To Speak Up In Meetings

The Challenge: Quiet Meetings
Does that sound like a problem? Perhaps you're thinking *Quiet? That sounds good, we can get through this faster and be done!* But if you've bothered to schedule a meeting, instead of just sending out information to be read, you probably have agenda issues that need input from others.

Good participation in meetings can be beneficial in many ways. Participants come away more engaged and energized. New ideas may be generated. New information may help you avoid mistakes. People will be more committed when they have participated in decision making.

Research by Alex Pentland, director of MIT's Human Dynamics Laboratory, confirms the importance of group and one-on-one communication among team members. Specifically, he finds that the most successful teams engage in face-to-face conversations where everyone contributes their "fair share" of "brief, to-the-point" comments.[1]

The Question: How Can You Get the Most Productive Meeting Participation?
You do need a meeting, right? Just checking.

Consider This

"I not only use all the brains I have, but all I can borrow."
—Woodrow Wilson

"Combining everyone's knowledge begets more knowledge, the way combining rice and beans begets more protein."
—Elizabeth Hilts

Try This: Encourage Meeting Participation Ten Ways

To get the best contribution from the broadest range of participants, try these strategies:

1) **Invite the Right People**
   Include participants who have a genuine need or interest in the agenda. Make sure they understand the role they are expected to play in the meeting. (*I know this is an issue for you and I'm hoping you can contribute x.*)

2) **Involve Them In Advance**
   Send out a meeting agenda and materials enough in advance to allow for preparation. If appropriate, let participants add to it. Be clear on the exact preparation needed, including what the participants need to send in advance or bring with them.

3) **Set Up to Encourage Participation**
   Schedule the meeting when people will be able to concentrate. For instance, don't schedule it during the middle of another crisis, when people are pushing to meet another important deadline, or when they are likely to be hungry or tired.

   Participants may be more comfortable speaking up if they know others in the room. If they don't already know each other, consider ways to help them connect and establish common ground beforehand or at the beginning of the meeting.

   Encourage discussion by seating participants where they can establish eye contact. If participation is important, specify time in the agenda for it. Let people know what kind of participation you want.

4) **Borrow Effective Meeting Facilitation Techniques**
   Sometimes participants are hesitant to speak up in the presence of higher-ranking participants or wait to see what higher-ups say first. (Consider that when you send out invitations.) If you want fresh ideas, you might ask bosses to hold back on sharing their opinions initially.

   To counter the effect of "meeting hogs" who dominate the conversation, consider using a "round robin" technique to give everyone a chance to contribute. (*To get a feel for where we are, let's go around the room to give each person a chance to briefly share their suggestions [concerns, reaction, etc.]. Let's try to keep it to a minute or so each. Who'd like to start?*)

   If issues are sensitive, use a secret ballot or have participants submit comments or questions via note cards to be collected and read by the facilitator.

5) **Ask Questions Skillfully**
Ask "Open" questions to start a discussion and welcome contributions. (*What is important here? How can we ... ? Why?*)

Then zero in on specifics with "Closed" questions, ones that usually have brief specific answers. (*Which? When? Where? Who?*)

When you ask, pause and lean back a little. Give people a chance to think and answer.

6) **Challenge the Crowd**
Are people stuck or drifting? Consider provoking a response. For instance, ask a penetrating question. *What's the real issue here? What's the fear?* Encourage bigger thinking. *What if anything were possible?* Or borrow a creative problem-solving technique by purposefully asking an outrageous question to get ideas flowing. For instance, deliberately reverse your direction. If you were looking for ways to get new customers, then, you might ask "How could we lose more customers?" (Note: To avoid misunderstanding or strange looks, you might announce your strategy. *I'm playing "devil's advocate"* or *Let's play with this by going way out there for a minute.*)

7) **Allow for Processing Time**
Some participants will want a little time to think through issues before reacting publicly. Others like to talk it through before they come to a conclusion. With important issues, build in some processing time such as short breaks between presentation of information and a call for responses; a few moments to think, reflect, or jot a few notes; or a lunch break before a big decision.

8) **Make It Safe**
"I've learned to keep my mouth shut." That's one of the reactions I hear from people who don't contribute in meetings. They've been stung—punished, laughed at, put down, criticized, demoted, or ignored. If you want people to speak up, they have to feel it's safe.

So ... what happens to people in your organization who tell the truth or ask questions? What can you do to shift your culture so people feel it's OK to speak up?

What happens when someone makes a suggestion that's not fully formed, a little off, or outright ridiculous? Does your face show disapproval? If so, you may be inadvertently dampening participation. Try ways to keep the conversation moving productively without embarrassing the contributor. Help them flesh out the idea. (*Let me see if I can help—is the issue* x? Anyone want to add to [or react to] that?} Or smoothly redirect the conversation. (*Thank you. Other thoughts?*)

9) **So What?**

   "They've already decided, so why bother?" "We talk and talk and nothing ever happens."

   Meeting participants often feel their input went into a big black hole. They contributed their time, thought, and energy and then nothing happened.

   Be clear on what you will do with input. For instance, are the participants making the decision? Or are you just checking your instincts?

   Will their input be recorded and shared elsewhere? If so, show later what happened with their suggestions. If appropriate, explain how a conclusion was reached on a decision for which they provided input.

10) **Get Some Fresh Air**

    Are people quiet because they're falling asleep? Turn up the lights; open the windows; turn the thermostat down a tad. Don't serve food that will induce naps. Stand up. Move around. Get real. Ask a few unexpected questions. Add some humor and stir.

Apply & Evaluate: What Do You Notice?

Try these techniques and notice what happens:
- *Did you get more participation? Broader participation? Better ideas?*
- *What else could you do to make meetings more productive?*
- *Why would someone benefit from speaking up at your meetings?*

Take Action: Now What?

Continue to add to your leadership skill by learning techniques for facilitating different types of meetings. Consider further ways to reshape your meeting culture so people actually look forward to the next one.

46) Eight Ways To Accomplish More In Less Meeting Time

The Challenge: Runaway Meetings
One of the top workplace gripes is "too much time spent in meetings." Specifically, workers complain about long meetings that accomplish little, meetings that get off track, and long-winded colleagues.

The Question: How Can You Keep Meetings In Check?
One way is simply to cut down on meetings. Before you schedule that meeting, ask yourself if a meeting is necessary. Is there a more efficient way to get something done?

> **Consider This**
>
> *"Meetings are indispensable when you don't want to do anything."*
> —John Kenneth Galbraith

Try This: Stay In Control
To accomplish more in less meeting time, employ these eight strategies:

1) **Define Your Outcome**
   Be clear on the outcome you want from the meeting; design the meeting agenda and process to achieve that. What do you want to come away with at the end? Ideas to investigate further? An understanding of issues? Changed behaviors? A specific decision? A plan? A process?

2) **Prepare to Move**
   Prepare people, prepare information, and prepare process so you can move quickly.

Let people know what to expect and how to prepare. Provide an agenda, participation list, and guidelines, including time limits and formats for presentations. Specify expected preparation. If appropriate, clue participants in on big issues to give them time to think them through or discuss them with others in advance.

What's needed to make a decision? Gather and prepare information in an easily-digestible format. Get agreement on direction and decision criteria from higher-ups if needed. Check in with gatekeepers, people who can block you or say no, to make sure you are set up to move ahead. Obtain approvals and resources you will need.

Different types of meetings require different processes. Given your desired outcome, what process will get you there smoothly? What format will your output take? What potential obstacles or issues can you anticipate? Plan your agenda and process to achieve your outcome most efficiently.

3) Ask "Who Really Needs to Be Here?"

There are times when it's ideal to include a lot of people in a meeting. For instance, "town hall" meetings allow you to get in front of a large number of people and hear a broad range of opinions. By expanding meeting participation, you may be providing an opportunity for participants to learn by listening to others. You could be accessing a greater diversity of experience. You might be helping to create a more inclusive community.

Generally, though, don't involve more people in the meeting than needed. The amount of time it will take to come to a decision will be in proportion to the number of people involved.

One question to ask before inviting more people is "Will more people make us smarter or dumber?" Sometimes involving more people dumbs down the process by unnecessarily slowing things down or leading to "group-think," where the easiest path is to just go with the crowd.

This is not to say you shouldn't get broad input for your decision. There are a number of ways you might solicit input from stakeholders before your official meeting. Ask. Survey. Hold a "Meeting Before the Meeting" or a "town hall."

If all you'll need from a participant is a specific piece of information or discrete reaction, consider asking them to be "on call" to give you that, rather than asking them to sit through the entire meeting. Contact them during a break or ask them to step in at the appropriate time.

4) **Consider Specialized Help**
To accomplish the best results in major meetings, consider bringing in a meeting facilitator. A facilitator manages the process, while allowing you to focus on the meeting content. A good facilitator will help you design and set up an effective meeting process, keep everyone focused, manage the time, ensure good participation, move the process forward, record output, and define any follow-up process—all while remaining neutral on the content and decisions.

5) **Don't Punish Good Behavior**
Don't punish the people who showed up on time by delaying the start of the meeting to accommodate chronic latecomers. Don't punish the people who came prepared by going over the details of material that should have been read before the meeting. Don't punish good listeners by repeating information people missed because they were talking or texting under the table.

This may require reshaping your meeting culture. Let people know the ground rules. *We won't have a meeting unless one is needed. We expect you to arrive prepared. We'll start on time. To keep the meeting as short as possible, we ask for your full attention.*

6) **Be Ready to Control Runaways**
Got colleagues who like to hear themselves talk? Consider using one of these techniques to keep meeting hogs under control:
- Use nonverbal signals to discourage them. Limit eye contact. Move toward someone else.
- Impose time limits on comments.
- Ask others to contribute.
- Thank them and redirect the conversation.

When tempted to digress, save off-topic issues in a "parking lot" instead. That is, acknowledge their importance by putting them on a list of issues to discuss at a different time. Be ready to steer the meeting back on course.

7) **Lead the Way**
Help people learn how to contribute productively by modeling productive input. Show that you've done your homework. Use constructive language. Turn gripes into requests or solutions by reflecting them back as questions, such as "What would work here?" or "What's the request?"

8) **Frustrated? Take a Break**
    If your meeting is stalled, consider stopping to do a quick check-in. For instance, you might say, "I want to pause for a few minutes to take our temperature. Let's quickly go around the room—let us know in 25 words or less where you stand at this point." That may provide some direction on how best to proceed.

    Another option is to take a break or table your issue, agreeing to come back to it at a specific time and noting specific steps that need to be taken in the interim.

Apply & Evaluate: What Do You Notice?
Try these strategies in your next round of meetings. Then consider:
- *What worked for your group?*
- *What else can you do to improve your group's meeting productivity?*
- *What, if any, shifts are needed in your culture to support effective meeting behaviors?*

Take Action: Now What?
Remember that process can be as important as content in determining your meeting outcome. Watch effective meeting facilitators and leaders. Learn techniques for running specific types of meetings and continue to improve this important leadership skill through practice.

47 Can We Just Talk?: When To Stop Arguing And Dialogue Instead

The Challenge: You're Not Getting Anywhere
You're in a rut. You need some new ideas. Arguing isn't getting you anywhere. Most people have checked out of the conversation.

The Question: How Can You Open Up New Possibilities?

> **Consider This**
>
> *"I believe we can change the world if we start listening to one another again. Simple, honest, human conversation. Not mediation, negotiation, problem-solving, debate, or public meetings. Simple, truthful conversation where we each have a chance to speak, we each feel heard, and we each listen well."*
> —Margaret J. Wheatley, *Turning to One Another*

Try This: Dialogue
Face it—there's a lot of pressure these days to get things done. One of the biggest meeting gripes is that they go on and on and nothing is decided.

Many of the most important problems we need to solve and opportunities we could leverage aren't ready for action, though. We need to open our minds. We need to understand each other. We need to explore.

The Limits of "The Argument Culture"
Not only are we under time pressure to make decisions and take action, we are often under pressure to prove ourselves, "win," and be "right." Our education system sets us up to think and communicate in this mode; it's reinforced by the press, politicians, and lawyers. In her book *The Argument Culture*, linguist

Deborah Tannen uses the phrase "culture of critique" to describe how we use criticism, attack, or opposition as the predominant ways of responding to people or ideas.[1]

This mode creates Winners and Losers, with scenarios that unwittingly limit us to Yes/No, Right/Wrong answers, instead of encouraging us to explore all sides and develop new options.

Another Option: Dialogue
Under certain circumstances, another more collaborative option may be productive: Dialogue. The term "dialogue" translates from Greek as "meaning flowing through." Organizational strategist William Isaacs calls it "the art of thinking together."

A dialogue provides a safe space for genuine exchange of ideas and opinions. There is neither a formal agenda nor an expectation of an end product, conclusion, or solution. Rather, it is an exchange in which exploration is encouraged, differences are welcome, and listening is vital. Systems scientist Peter Senge describes such conversations as having "a 'life of their own,' taking us in directions we could never have imagined nor planned in advance."[2] Such conversations may lead to new ideas, change, improved understanding, and increased trust.

"In true dialogue, both sides are willing to change."

—Thich Nhat Hanh

Debate vs. Dialogue
As Deborah Tannen notes, our culture frequently sets us up for a debate-like exchange. Debate and Dialogue are different in several significant ways:
- **Goal:** In a debate, the goal is to win. In a dialogue, the goal is to create understanding and meaning. A debate ends with a winner and a loser. Ideally, a dialogue ends with participants all "winning" greater perspective.
- **Mode:** In a debate, the participants are competing with each other. They defend their own positions and speak to persuade others they are right. Participants approach a dialogue with a neutral stance. They suspend judgment, listen to each other, and explore ideas.
- **Range:** A debate pits two points of view against each other, whereas, in a dialogue, multiple points of view may be entertained simultaneously.

When To Have a Dialogue
Dialogue can be useful in several situations, such as when a group:
- Is stuck or polarized on important issues.
- Faces large scale change.
- Needs to prepare to make important, complex decisions.
- Would benefit from a deeper level of exchange.

What Makes Dialogue Work
In *The Fifth Discipline, The Art and Practice of the Learning Organization*, Peter Senge identifies three basic requirements for effective dialogue:

1) All participants must "suspend" their assumptions.
2) All participants must regard one another as colleagues.
3) There must be a "facilitator" who "holds the context" of dialogue.[3]

A successful dialogue focuses on a greater purpose. It begins by looking for common ground or hopes. Participants:
- Are committed to the topic and to each other.
- Genuinely seek understanding.
- Come willing to listen deeply.
- Come willing to engage.
- Use "I" messages; that is, they refer to their own opinions, observations, feelings, or perspective (*From my perspective, I notice, I feel, I think, I believe*).
- Are comfortable with silence, if needed, to allow others to put their thoughts into words and for ideas to emerge.

Setting Up a Dialogue
To set up a productive dialogue, address these process elements:

Set Expectations: Indicate that the meeting is specifically intended to be a dialogue. The purpose will be to share perspectives, increase understanding, and exchange ideas. No specific outcome is expected.

Venue: A dialogue can take place anywhere. Set up the space so people can see each other. To show that fresh thinking is encouraged, consider holding the dialogue in a different space than your regular decision-making meetings.

Topic: Provide the topic in advance. Prepare a few thoughtful open-ended questions to get the dialogue started.

Format and Ground Rules: The specific dialogue format may vary depending on the nature of your topic, the size of the group, and their previous dialogue experience. It may range from a very freeform exchange to one with a defined process.

Consider guidelines for speakers. For instance, how will speakers take part? Will they just volunteer to speak up? Or will the dialogue flow around the room in "round robin" style? Will there be time limits for individual comments to ensure enough time for all to contribute? Will participants be allowed to address questions to other speakers?

Coming to Closure
When participants are accustomed to decision-producing meetings, it might feel strange to end the meeting without a specific resolution. Do acknowledge the benefits of the dialogue, such as increased clarity, an appreciation of honest reactions, information, or ideas you can work with further. End on a positive note, thanking participants for sharing. If appropriate, set up a time for follow-up.

Apply & Evaluate: What Do You Notice?
Consider possible applications of dialogue in your organization:
- *When would it be useful for your group to have a dialogue?*
- *How can you set up your dialogue to elicit the best participation?*
- *What positive byproducts might dialogue produce for your group?*

Take Action: Now What?
Dialogue adds an important collaboration and meeting option to your leadership toolkit. With experience, groups using dialogue learn deeper thinking and listening skills, which often transform relationships.

To explore the idea of dialogue further, see William Isaacs' *Dialogue: The Art of Thinking Together* and Peter Senge's *The Fifth Discipline: The Art and Practice of the Learning Organization.*

48 Moving Ideas Ahead: The BRAIN Process

The Challenge: What Happens (Or Doesn't) After Your Brainstorm

Good ideas often get stuck in process. They get smothered by critics before they have a chance to breathe. Potential benefits may be overlooked or fuzzy. On the other hand, sometimes we waste time debating fine points about potential implementation problems, when the idea isn't worth the trouble.

The Question: How Can You Develop and Move the Best Ideas Ahead?

Brainstorming sessions typically yield ideas that aren't complete, ideal, or workable. Most need some cultivation before they're ready to harvest.

Consider This

"Ideas are like rabbits. You get a couple and learn how to handle them and pretty soon you have a dozen."
—John Steinbeck

"Ideas are easy. Implementation is hard."
—Guy Kawasaki

Try This: The BRAIN Process

BRAIN stands for Benefits, Risks, Alternatives, Intuition, and Next Steps. When evaluating ideas, use this B-R-A-I-N process systematically to productively direct energy, streamline the process, and increase the likelihood of developing effective solutions. Focus on one step at a time.

Benefits:
Begin by noting only the benefits or potential benefits of the idea.
- *What's the major purpose of the idea?*
- *Who could benefit from it?*
- *What would the benefit be?*
- *How could the potential benefit be measured?*
- *What other hidden benefits might there be?*

Then ask:
- *Does this idea offer enough potential benefit to warrant investing time and energy to pursue it?*

If so, take the next step. If not, move on to the next idea, storing worthwhile remnants where they might be revisited at a different time.

Risks:
Most new ideas involve some risk or issues that need to be worked out. Identify as many as you can. Get them all out on the table. Ask:
- *What problems or issues does this raise?*
- *What are the potential risks or downsides?*

When you've identified all the potential issues or risks, identify significant ones by asking:
- *How big is the potential risk, downside, or problem?*
- *How likely is it?*

Alternatives:
Work through significant issues, looking for potential adjustments or alternative solutions:
- *What would have to happen or be in place for this idea to work?*
- *How could the potential risks be eliminated?*
- *If it's not possible to eliminate risks, how could they be minimized?*
- *How could issues of concern be handled?*
- *What alternatives are there?*
- *Is there another way to achieve the same benefit without the risk?*
- *Could the potential risk, downside, or issue be turned into an opportunity?*

Then, refine your idea. If needed, repeat these first three steps—Benefit, Risk, Alternatives—with your improved idea.

Intuition:
Now, besides thinking the idea through, step back and test it with your heart and gut:
- *How does it feel?*
- *How will others feel about it?*
- *What does your gut say about it?*

Pay attention to your intuition. Address any concerns by repeating relevant steps above.

Next Steps:
When you've culled and refined your best ideas, move ahead to outline your action plan:
- *What do we need to move this ahead?*
- *What actions should be taken next?*

Apply & Evaluate: What Do You Notice?
When your group is ready to evaluate ideas, try the BRAIN process. Then note:
- *How was the quality of your harvest?*
- *How did focusing on one aspect at a time (e.g. Benefits, Risks, Alternatives) affect your efficiency?*
- *How did using this process affect teamwork and relationships?*

Take Action: Now What?
Work with this process and other collaborative tools to increase the quality, quantity, and efficiency of your group's output. While it may take some practice, meeting processes such as this can make a significant difference in your output.

49) Your Influence Map: Who You Need To Know To Get Things Done

The Challenge: Getting Things Done
When you need to get things done in an organization, you don't always have total control. Some will do what you ask or demand because you are their boss, but you'll often need to get agreement, ideas, or action from others over whom you have no control.

The Question: Whose Trust, Support, Resources, Cooperation, and Attention Do You Need?
To increase your organizational effectiveness, recognize the support you might need to get things done; cultivate healthy, mutually beneficial relationships *before* you need help.

Consider This

"The key to successful leadership today is influence, not authority."
—Kenneth Blanchard

Try This: Your Influence Map

Organizational Charts vs. Influence Maps
Take a blank sheet of paper and draw an organizational chart showing formal reporting relationships for your part of your organization.

Now, think through how things *really* get done. Consider one of your most important projects or goals. Along with those with whom you are formally related on the "org chart" (e.g. your boss and subordinates), whose help do you need?:

- *Who has valuable skills or expertise?*
- *Who has access to information and resources?*
- *Who can call upon a large or influential network?*
- *Who is an "opinion leader" whose support can be helpful in moving new ideas forward?*
- *Who is a "gatekeeper" who can say no or block important access?*
- *Who has formal power (i.e. power because of position or title)?*
- *Who has informal power (i.e. power because of who they are, whom they know, or how they operate)?*
- *Whose support do you need to implement your plan or project?*
- *With whom would your boss say it's important for you to have a relationship?*

Also, consider your influence on others:
- *Who has a stake in your success?*
- *Who needs your help to move their ideas and projects forward?*
- *Who is a natural connection?*

Now, on a separate sheet, draw an "Influence Map" showing important informal relationships:

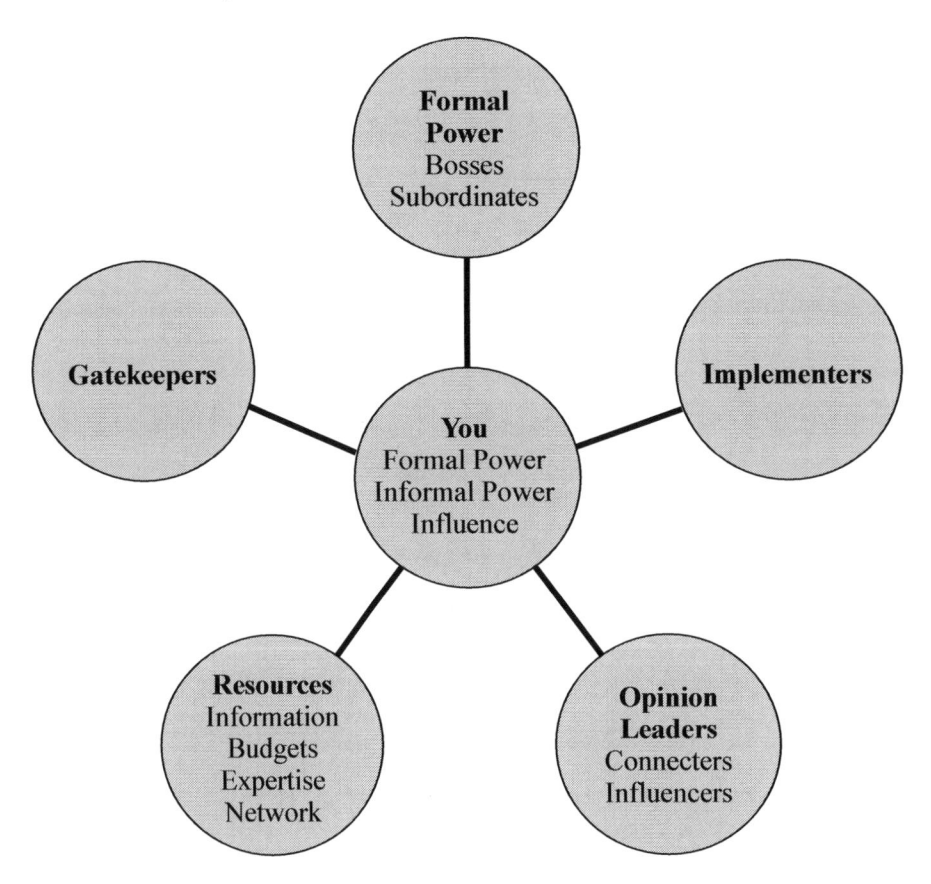

Formal Power
Bosses
Subordinates

Gatekeepers

Implementers

You
Formal Power
Informal Power
Influence

Resources
Information
Budgets
Expertise
Network

Opinion Leaders
Connecters
Influencers

Cultivate Relationships

Make an effort to cultivate relationships with those on your Influence Map. Get to know these individuals personally. Find out what's important to them. Learn about their challenges. Offer support when appropriate.

"Off the Chart" Opportunities

Relationships that extend your reach beyond the formal organizational chart can be beneficial to both you and your organization.

Performance improvement conversations in organizations typically take place up and down hierarchical lines. Bosses work with their own subordinates to spot problems within their departments, plan, make improvements, evaluate progress, and make further adjustments. Because of their formal reporting relationships, there is a high level of control.

Departmental managers can only go so far by themselves, however. Many of the biggest problems in organizations take place "between the cracks." That is, the problems happen in the processes that occur between departments. If you have cultivated relationships beyond your own department, you will be more apt to be effective in working through such problems. This can be politically sensitive ground, because accountability is less clear; there is a tendency to defend one's turf and actions. (It can be easier ground to forge when a specific assignment has been given.) Strong peer relationships create a good foundation for this type of work.

"Between the Cracks" Conversations

"Managing sideways" by being a leader among your peers can be both challenging and rewarding.

Successful "between the cracks" conversations require trust. Look for mutual benefits to making improvements. Respect your colleagues' turf. Include them in conversations and decisions that affect them and their team members. Earn their trust by delivering on your promises and by making them look good.

Ask for their opinions and listen deeply. Invite collaboration (*If there were a way to ... , would you be interested?*). Question respectfully (*To what extent is this an issue for you?*). Acknowledge that things may look different from their viewpoint (*From my perspective, ... How does it look from your perspective?*).

Apply & Evaluate: What Do You Notice?

Notice what you can achieve when you have already established a relationship with someone on your Influence Map before you need something.

Then consider:
- *What improvement opportunities lie "between the cracks"?*
- *How might you approach these?*
- *How can you continue to expand your circle of influence?*

Take Action: Now What?

Your relationships and ability to influence others will be increasingly important as you move up in organizations. Keep expanding your circle. Develop strong communication and influence skills. Build trust and support to move ideas and projects forward and get things done.

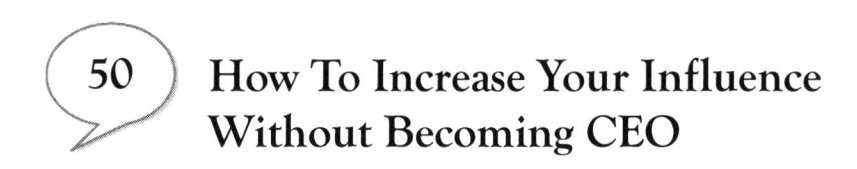

50 How To Increase Your Influence Without Becoming CEO

The Challenge: Influencing Others or Events When You Don't Have a Big, Fancy Title

Influence is defined as *"the capacity to have an effect on the character, development, or behavior of someone or something."*

The Question: How Can You Be More Influential?

Do you want others to listen to you? Do you want to make a difference? No matter where you are on the organizational chart, you can build your capacity to affect others and events.

> **Consider This**
>
> *"Power is a tool, influence is a skill; one is a fist, the other a fingertip."*
> —Nancy Gibbs

Try This: Identify and Develop Your Sources of Influence

Have you noticed people who achieve influence beyond their formal positions? People regularly turn to them for input and advice. They can often be identified by asking "Who influences the decision maker?" Sometimes they are described with terms such as "the architect," "the brains behind ... ," "an insider," "a power broker," or "a connector."

The amount of influence one wields is situational. It will change from opportunity to opportunity depending on factors such as level of relevant expertise and reputation with the players involved. There are, however, factors that can increase one's overall level of influence.

Factors That Increase Influence

Two of the most obvious factors people think of when they identify influence are position and title. If these reflect power and credibility, others are more likely to pay attention.

Additional factors—skill, resources, relationships, information, personal qualities, and reputation—may be a little less obvious, but provide a basis from which one can wield significant influence.

Consider these specific factors that determine and enhance one's level of potential influence:

- **"Track record"**: Past contributions and successes
- **Reputation**: What one is known for. Perceptions of one's competence and character.
- **Expertise**: Special knowledge and skill
- **Resources**: Financial resources, information, equipment, tools, staff, and other resources
- **Interpersonal skill**: Ability to establish rapport, gain trust, and communicate effectively
- **Network**: Whom one knows and can easily call upon
- **Connections**: Power one can deliver through alliances, leverage, or inside knowledge
- **Trustworthiness**: Perception that one can be counted on to deliver, to keep confidences, and to consider others' needs and interests
- **Influence characteristics**: Persuasiveness, negotiation ability, motivation, energy level, and appearance of success
- **Other value**: Other potential value the individual brings to a particular situation

Which ones could you cultivate and leverage to increase your influence?

Apply & Evaluate: What Do You Notice?

Observe people who seem to have influence that exceeds their formal authority. Notice:

- *How do they achieve this influence?*
- *Which of their effective behaviors and qualities could you develop?*
- *Which, if any, behaviors or qualities would you want to avoid taking on?*

Take Action: Now What?

If you want to make a difference beyond your formal position, cultivate skills, resources, relationships, information, personal qualities, and a reputation that will increase your credibility and power.

51) How To Influence Someone

The Challenge: A Big Pitch
You want to make a change or a difference. You want to affect behavior, character, or development. Or you've got something to sell—a product, an idea, or yourself.

The Question: How Can You Influence Someone?
In preparing to write his 2012 book, *To Sell is Human*, Daniel Pink commissioned research that asked a sample of more than 7,000 full-time U.S. workers how they spend their time at work. His findings: "People are now spending about 40 percent of their time at work engaged in non-sales selling—persuading, influencing, and convincing others in ways that don't involve anyone making a purchase." Moreover, he found that influence and sales skills were the ones that made the biggest difference in their level of success.[1]

To some degree, we're all in sales.

> **Consider This**
>
> *"Always be sure to influence another in a way that ensures that you haven't damaged your ability to influence this person again in the future. In other words, the other person must benefit from the change you've created."*
> –Robert Cialdini

Try This: Know the Person You Are Trying to Influence
First, before we talk about the person you want to influence, look inside.

Who Has Influenced You?
Think of someone who has had a big influence on you.
- *Why were they, in particular, able to influence you?*
- *What did they do?*
- *How did it feel?*
- *What did it mean to you?*

Then, most importantly:
- *Would you accept their influence again?*
- *If so, what makes you open to their ongoing influence? If not, why not?*

Consider your reactions. It's likely that others will react similarly when you attempt to influence them.

Why Should They Listen to You?
Unless you have something truly of benefit to the person you are trying to influence, stop now. You might have some temporary success, but the tactics you would have to use would likely backfire at some point. You're unlikely to get a solid commitment by using guilt or forcing people to do things. Manipulation breeds resentment. By itself, logic only goes so far. Dishonesty causes bigger problems.

You must have something of benefit to offer. People must truly feel something is right to enthusiastically commit to it long-term.

Trust Comes First
To accept your influence, others must be willing to trust you. For there to be deep trust, the other person must believe 1) you are competent and able to deliver, 2) you are true to your word and *will* deliver, and 3) you have their best interests at heart.

Trust is earned over time. If you already have a relationship, the level of trust will depend on past experience. If you're new to each other, you may have to work at building some trust first.

Influence = Benefit + Trust + Knowing the Person You Are Dealing With
Your ability to influence another person increases as you know more about them and what's important to them, as that helps you fully recognize and successfully convey the specific benefit you have to offer.

How Will You Be Able to Know Them?
As their level of trust in you increases, the amount and type of information others are willing to disclose increases and deepens. For instance, their level of disclosure might deepen like this:
- "Small talk"
- Facts
- Preferences
- Needs and Interests
- Opinions
- Values
- Feelings
- Emotions

Steps you can take to increase another person's level of disclosure include these:
1) Make the other person comfortable.
2) Cultivate trust.
3) Volunteer some information and encourage a response.
4) Recognize and adapt to individual styles and preferences regarding disclosure. One who normally sticks to facts may need help articulating feelings, while one who is more comfortable divulging feelings may need help recognizing facts.
5) Ask questions. Get a reaction. Listen fully.

Uncovering Values
One key to influencing another person is recognizing what that person values. You might ask, "What's most important to you?"

Since the person you'd like to influence may not have specifically thought about his or her values or be able to succinctly articulate them, here are three ways to spot another's likely values:
1) **Watch their "walk"**—how they invest their time, energy, money, and other resources.
2) **Pay attention to the underlying elements of their "talk"**—topics, tone, and language. What topics do they gravitate toward? Notice shifts of vocal tone that reveal what they get excited about. What "gets them going"? Listen to what's emphasized in their language.
3) **Watch for what's important to them.** What are their priorities and aspirations? Of what do they seem most proud?

Careful observation and listening for this evidence, either in the context of life or career (or both), can help you quickly gauge another's values.

Addressing Needs

Additionally, try to determine what the other person needs. Needs are different from values. What MUST they have? What does that look like to them?

Consider both professional needs and personal needs. For instance, someone's professional needs might be one of these:
- To complete a project
- To make a profit
- To negotiate a low price
- To produce a quality product
- To be recommended
- To receive funding

Personal needs might be one or more of these:
- To feel safe
- To feel successful
- To save face
- To feel accepted

What's the other person's need generally? What is it in relation to your issue? How will they measure success or decide what's right for them? Uncover as much as you can about their needs through research, observation, and skillful questioning. Then, focus on the aspects of your proposal that meet their needs. Target your message to address what's important to them. For instance, if their major need is financial, focus on the numbers. If it's safety, consider offering a guarantee or focus on other ways you can reduce risk for them.

Ideally, they'll tell you their need or there will be some evidence of it. Sometimes you have to make an assumption; be alert and ready to shift in case you weren't spot on.

How Do They Like It Served Up?

Think of a favorite restaurant. The server knows exactly how you like your meal served. He steers you to a quiet table. He brings your drink of choice automatically when you sit down. He doesn't make you wait a long time between courses. He knows you want dressing on the side or a little extra sauce. It sure makes a difference, doesn't it? If he made a recommendation on what was good on tonight's menu, you'd listen, right?

Knowing something about how the person you want to influence likes to be approached can smooth your way, too. As you prepare, consider practical ways to set things up to flow easily.

For instance, consider:
- *How does this person like to receive information? Do they prefer a face-to-face meeting, or would they rather receive a written proposal? Do they prefer a text, an email, or a phone call?*
- *Do they want to see a lot of detail or just the major points?*
- *Do they need time to think things over?*
- *What are their "hot buttons," i.e. what do they focus on first and most?*

It Comes Back to Trust

Never forget the importance of trust. No one likes to be tricked or manipulated. As they say, "Fool me once, shame on you. Fool me twice, shame on me." For the long haul, trust is imperative.

Apply & Evaluate: What Do You Notice?

When you want to influence someone, prepare by identifying:
- *What do they value?*
- *What do they need?*
- *What do you have to offer that would be of benefit to them?*
- *How can you build trust?*
- *How do they like to be approached?*

Afterward, assess:
- *Were your assumptions correct? If not, were you ready to adjust?*
- *What can you do to increase your influence with this person and in this situation?*
- *How are you most easily influenced by others?*

Take Action: Now What?

Think back to the person you identified earlier who greatly influenced you. If you were able to influence others in that way, what would the impact be? Increase your ability to make a difference by continuing to develop your relationships and influence skills.

DEVELOPING TEAMS & TALENT

52 Your Strengths Strategy

The Challenge: Standing Out In a Crowded World
You want to stand out in a *good* way, of course.

The Question: How Can You Shine?
Figure out what you do best and use your strengths to excel.

> **Consider This**
>
> *"A leader needs to know his strengths as a carpenter knows his tools, or as a physician knows the instruments at her disposal. What great leaders have in common is that each truly knows his or her strengths—and can call on the right strength at the right time. This explains why there is no definitive list of characteristics that describes all leaders."*
> —Dr. Donald O. Clifton, *Strengths Based Leadership*

Try This: Your Strengths Strategy
Follow these three Strengths Strategy steps:
    1) Identify Your Strengths
    2) Develop Your Strengths
    3) Leverage Your Strengths

Two Types of Strengths
Each of us possesses a unique combination of strengths—qualities, aptitudes, skills, and capacities in which we excel. These strengths include natural strengths, ones we are "born with," as well as developed strengths, ones we have developed through education or experience.

Identify Your Strengths

The first step in developing your strengths is recognizing them. To uncover the fullest view of your strengths, use a combination of three methods: self-evaluation, assessments, and feedback.

1) **Self-Evaluation**

    What do *you* consider to be your strengths?
    - *What do you think you do well?*
    - *What comes easily to you?*
    - *What do you notice or pay attention to that others don't?*
    - *When have you been most successful?*
    - *What uniqueness sets you apart?*
    - *What special expertise and talents have you developed?*

2) **Assessments**

    Formal assessments can provide additional perspective on strengths. Examples of these are:
    - The *Clifton StrengthsFinder®*, an assessment developed by Donald Clifton and his colleagues at The Gallup Organization that identifies your five areas of greatest talent among 34 profile areas.
    - The *Myers Briggs Type Indicator®*, which identifies your most natural ways of thinking and acting—how you get energy, what you notice first and most, how you approach decisions, and how you organize your life. A good interpretation of this assessment will include identification of probable natural strengths and contributions.

3) **Feedback**

    Feedback from others can be invaluable. Sometimes we miss seeing our strengths because they are so natural to us that we assume they are also natural to everyone else.
    - What have your managers, teachers, or coaches identified as strengths?
    - What have others told you "Oh, you're so good at … "?
    - Ask friends, family members, and colleagues what they think your strengths are.

Developing Strengths

Next, take these steps to develop your strengths:

1) **Analyze**

    Build confidence by figuring out how your strengths work. Step back and ask yourself:
    - *How exactly do I do that?*
    - *What's unique about the way I do that?*
    - *How can I replicate that or teach it to others?*

2) **Manage**

    Once you recognize how you operate using your strengths, you can regulate when and how you use them. Notice where and how you can contribute through your strengths. Avoid overusing them or using them at inappropriate times. Recognize when others might need you to slow down, explain, or give an example of things that seem easy to you, but might not be to them.

3) **Develop**

    Cultivate your strengths further through additional education and experience.

Leverage Your Strengths and Thrive!

Using your strengths allows you to shine and become known for your unique "personal brand." According to research by The Gallup Group, workers who get to use their strengths are also significantly more engaged at work.[1]

Look for opportunities to exercise your strengths:
- *Where and how are you currently using your strengths?*
- *How could you further employ them? For instance ...*

    ... on the job

    ... in your organization

    ... in your community

    ... with your family or friends

- *How aware are others of your strengths? If they're not already, how could they become aware?*

Caution: Strengths as Weaknesses
Enjoy developing and using your strengths, but don't go overboard! Richard Farson puts it well in *Management of the Absurd*: "Strengths can become weaknesses when we rely too much on them, carry them to exaggerated lengths, or apply them where they don't belong. The stronger they are, the more likely they are also to be weaknesses."[2]

What About Weaknesses?
Generally one can get a better and faster "ROI," return on investment, by developing strengths than by shoring up weaknesses. Some deficiencies, however, can't be ignored. Know what's important in your role and the roles to which you aspire. Work to bring required weak skills up to standards.

Apply & Evaluate: What Do You Notice?
Identify your top strengths. Then, strategize:
- *How can you continue to develop your strengths?*
- *Which strengths contribute most to your "brand"? Where else can you employ them?*
- *How can you prevent your strengths from becoming liabilities?*

Take Action: Now What?
Now that you've identified your strengths, find ways to further cultivate them.

As a leader, encourage those around you to identify, develop, and apply their strengths, as well.

53 Beyond Potential: How To Develop Your Talents

The Challenge: The Burden of Potential

You can lose your job or wallet, but no one can take away your talent. Your talent isn't worth much, though, unless it is cultivated and put to use. Developed talents can create confidence, career advantages, and satisfaction. Others may provide encouragement, but your development is ultimately up to you.

The Question: What Can You Do to Develop Your Talents?

Consider This

"There's nothing heavier than the burden of potential."
—Snoopy

"Mastering others is strength. Mastering yourself is true power."
—Lao Tzu

"To every person there comes in their lifetime that special moment when you are figuratively tapped on the shoulder and offered the chance to do a very special thing, unique to you and your talents. What a tragedy if that moment finds you unprepared or unqualified for the work which could have been your finest hour."
—Winston Churchill

Try This: Talent Development Strategies

Apply these principles and strategies used in fields as diverse as the arts, athletics, and business to develop your own talents:

Know Yourself

Each of us possesses a unique set of capabilities and preferences. Identify yours, work with them, and use them to your advantage.

Know where you shine. One musician might be technically brilliant, while another creates a special connection with the audience. While both must develop an adequate level of must-have technical and performance skill, each has a particular way to stand out. They will thrive in roles where their individual strengths are especially valued. If your strengths are not obvious to you, ask respected colleagues and friends for feedback. Consider not only what you already do well or what comes naturally, but areas of undeveloped potential.

Figure out how you learn best. Do you prefer learning in a group, where you can interact and learn from others; or by yourself, so you can concentrate deeply and focus on specific areas of interest? If in a group, do you prefer one that is competitive or one that is supportive? Do you learn best by reading, by lecture, by observing, or just by experimenting? To make best use of your learning time and energy, choose the methods that are most effective for you.

Know Your Why

It takes commitment, time, and energy to become really good at something. You're probably already swamped, so you'll need to have a good reason to get going and keep going. *What is your purpose for developing your talent right now?* It might be a comprehensive long-term vision of how you want to use your gifts to make the world a better place or it might be the nearer-term goal of being able to get a better job. The most important thing is that it is YOUR reason. Others —a boss, a spouse, a competitor, or a friend—might express their opinions of what you should do and why, but, ultimately, the spark must come from within.

Write Down Goals

To focus your energy, time, and activities, write down goals. *What outcomes are you aiming for? What will success look like?* Use two timeframes—one long-term, to give you something big and inspiring to work toward; and one near-term, to give you something very concrete to accomplish on the way to that greater goal. Stretch yourself a bit, while still choosing achievable goals.

Set Yourself Up to Progress
Take steps to increase your learning effectiveness:

Write out your development plan. Include your purpose, goals, learning methods, and evaluation criteria.

Schedule learning activities. Along with larger, concentrated blocks of time, be ready to use spare moments for reading, observing, reviewing, practicing, or other learning activities. If you get off schedule, have a plan to resume quickly.

Apply your learning right away. Use more than one method in your learning and, most importantly, choose at least one active method. For example, read and then apply your learning through a project. Attend a lecture and then present the key principles you learned to someone else.

Build skill. Focus on learning or improving 1–2 things at a time. Practice those until you are "unconsciously competent"—that is, you do them automatically without having to think about it. Then move to higher-level skills and combinations of skills.

Get support. Share your goals and plan with others who will provide encouragement and help you keep on track.

Accelerate Learning
To learn most efficiently, follow these seven guidelines:

1) **Learn Principles:** Look for the principles underlying your area of development. If you can learn the basics, it's likely that you can progress quickly. For instance, to become a good singer, learn the principles of good breathing, the foundation of good singing. To become a good salesperson, learn the principles of asking effective questions.

2) **Practice High-Impact Skills:** Identify the sub-skills and factors that will produce the biggest improvement. Concentrate your efforts on developing the areas that count most. For example, in leadership development, keen self-awareness and masterful presentation skills significantly boost overall effectiveness.

3) **Practice Effectively:** Practice mindfully. Don't just go through the motions. Practice makes permanent, so practice doing things right. Otherwise, you are just reinforcing poor form and habits. Drill the hard

parts, the significant parts, and the parts that need the most improvement. Spend most of your practice time and energy there first; then put it all together in context. Add some fun to your practice sessions by creating a game or challenge for yourself.

4) **Find a Good Teacher or Mentor:** Work with someone skilled in your area of development who "gets" you, your goals, and your organization or field. In choosing the right person, consider not only their expertise, but their skill in teaching and their motivation to help you progress.

5) **Learn to Self-Evaluate:** A good teacher will help you learn to evaluate yourself when they're not around. Know when you're "doing it right" and how to get useful feedback.

6) **Expand Your Repertoire:** Observe a range of experts in your area of development. Watch, listen, and learn. Consider what each does well and what would work for you.

7) **Access Resources:** The internet makes it easy to research resources aligned with your learning preferences, whether that leads you to books, podcasts, forums, networking groups, online classes, or places to volunteer your services as you learn.

Do It!
The best and fastest way to develop any talent is to get experience. For instance, take on a new project, find a problem and solve it, or apply your skills in a new arena. Nothing substitutes for action.

Keep Stretching
Talent development is a constant process. As you progress, you find that more is possible. Those who have developed their talents most have consistently pushed themselves toward higher levels of performance. Challenge yourself to take a step out of your comfort zone. Consider trying something when you're 80-90% ready, instead of waiting until everything's perfect. If you're afraid of potential serious consequences of failing, take a few risks in front of a safe audience or take on a project outside of your normal sphere as a volunteer.

Keep a Fresh Outlook
Sometimes experts become complacent—or even miss big discoveries—because their history and schooling ironically prevent them from seeing things new ways. Make a point to deliberately look at the world with "fresh eyes."

Apply & Evaluate: What Do You Notice?
Make a plan for your own talent development:
- *Which talent do you feel most compelled to develop?*
- *What's the best way for you to go about that?*
- *Where will you apply that talent?*

Take Action: Now What?
Now go put your talents to good use!

Moreover, don't be a secret. It's not just what you can do, it's who knows you can do it.

54 ★ What About Weaknesses?

The Challenge: Our Weaknesses
No one excels at absolutely everything.

The Question: How Can You Best Manage Your Weaknesses?

> **Consider This**
>
> *"I think knowing what you cannot do is more important than knowing what you can."*
> —Lucille Ball
>
> *"I think the way I look at things gives me a different perspective. I'm most valuable when I work with a team of bright people who complement my weaknesses with their strengths."*
> —Craig McCaw

Try This: Got Weaknesses? Be Strategic!

Two Types of Weaknesses
Weaknesses fall into two categories:
1) **Lack of Awareness**: Some weaknesses are due to lack of exposure, education, or experience—you don't know what you don't know. This category also includes "blind spots"—gaps you can't see yourself. Such a weakness might be turned into competence if you become aware of it and are willing to take steps to improve.
2) **Areas of Difficulty**: These are skills or qualities that don't seem to come easily to you. While improvement can take place with awareness and effort, alternative strategies may be appropriate.

Sez Who?

Before you address something as a weakness, be sure it really is one. How did you decide it was a weakness? Sometimes we limit ourselves unnecessarily because of a bad experience or because we've been criticized. Before you accept a weakness because of criticism, consider the source. Is there actual evidence of a weakness, or is it someone's opinion or speculation? Sometimes criticism is as much a reflection of the criticizer as the criticized. Before you accept a weakness because of one bad incident, consider whether that may have been due to inexperience or an unusual series of events.

Should You Bother "Fixing" Your Weaknesses?

As noted in the earlier article on strengths, one can generally get a better and faster "ROI," return on investment, by developing strengths than by shoring up weaknesses. Some deficiencies can't be ignored, however. If needed, work to bring skills required in your job (or for the job to which you aspire) at least up to standards.

Got Weakness? Be Strategic

Once you've identified weaknesses, decide on the best strategy to address each:

> **Learning & Improving:** This strategy is best when learning and improving would be one or more of the following:
> - ✓ Easy
> - ✓ Systematic
> - ✓ Interesting
> - ✓ Required to reach minimum standards for your current and desired roles
>
> **Avoiding:** Can you avoid having to work with your weaknesses at all? For instance, if math is difficult for you, can you avoid quantitative roles?
>
> **Creating a System:** Can you, with help if needed, create a system to handle the weak function under most circumstances? For instance, can you create a template, formula, or process that happens automatically or with little additional effort on your part (e.g. setting up automatic bill payment or a spreadsheet with formulas that will automatically calculate the numbers you need)?
>
> **Partnering:** Can you collaborate with someone else who is strong where you are weak? Think of famous songwriting teams, such as Rodgers and

Hammerstein and Gilbert and Sullivan, where one wrote the words and the other the music.

Delegating: Can you delegate a major part of the function you're not good at? Then you'd primarily just have to recognize and be able to communicate what you need.

Outsourcing: Can you hire a third party with specific expertise to perform the function? You might be surprised at how cost-effective doing this can be either with local services or ones provided online through sites such as Fiverr or Elance.

Your Weakness as a Strength: Sometimes a trait may be a weakness in one context, but a strength in another. In one role, for instance, lack of attention to detail could be devastating, while in another role calling for big-picture thinking and broad strategy, it could be a plus. One situation might require deep, specific expertise, while a lack of it, allowing one to be able to approach a problem with "beginner eyes," may be an advantage where a fresh, creative approach is needed. If you can identify such situations, your "weakness" could be a strength.

Apply & Evaluate: What Do You Notice?
Take stock of your weaknesses. If needed, get feedback from trusted colleagues or friends who know you well. Then consider:
- *Which ones require personal improvement?*
- *In which cases would another strategy make sense?*
- *Which "weaknesses" might actually be strengths in certain situations?*

Take Action: Now What?
Don't limit yourself because of weaknesses; consider the best strategies for managing them. Address ones that require improvement to come up to standards for your current and future roles. Identify your strengths and focus most of your learning efforts on further developing those.

55 The "Feeling Factor"

The Challenge: Criticism Professional Women Hear: "You're too ... !"

Underneath successful, confident appearances, many bright female managers and leaders struggle with "fit" issues. As with men, some fit issues have to do with their fit in a particular position or organizational culture.

With women, however, the fit predicament is more complicated. I hear them say things such as *"I try hard to be both results-oriented and compassionate, but I can't seem to win. I get criticized by some for being too tough and by others for being too soft,"* or *"I fit in fine with the men, but have a hard time with many of the other women!"*

What's a woman to do? We attempt not only to fit in traditionally male-dominated cultures, but to accommodate diverse individual styles among both men and women.

The Question: How Can "Thinking Like a Woman" Work for You?

First, let's challenge the general assumption that there's a female way of thinking. Sometimes stereotypes apply; sometimes not. We're all a little different and, furthermore, we can all learn to apply different types of thinking.

That said, many women leaders struggle today because of a common female characteristic that may paradoxically give them a dramatic advantage in the work world of the future.

Consider This

"Mankind are governed more by their feelings than by reason."
—Samuel Adams

> "The stark conclusion that emerges from the work on group intelligence is that women make groups smarter ... the more women in a group, the smarter it is, plain and simple."
> —Geoff Colvin[1]
>
> "To handle yourself, use your head; to handle others, use your heart."
> —Eleanor Roosevelt

Try This: Know Your Natural Thinking Style. Flex When Needed.

One aspect of the "fit" issue for women is related to what I'll call "The Feeling Factor."

Consider the hypothetical scenario below:

> One day a manager, Susan, discovers that for the last six months an employee, John, has been taking $200 a month from a small business bank account to which they both have access. John is a well-liked, longtime employee with a solid performance record. When confronted, John admits that he has taken the money. He explains that he planned to return it as soon as he could, but his family has had some financial emergencies. His wife recently lost her job and one of the kids got very sick, causing them to accumulate unanticipated medical expenses.

What's your first reaction?
1) It's sad, but we've got to fire him right away. He's stolen from the company and we just can't tolerate that, OR
2) He's done wrong, but he's a good employee who's been in a difficult situation and he has agreed to return the money. Perhaps we can work with him.

Your first reaction likely indicates your natural decision-making mode. Katherine Briggs and her daughter, Isabel Briggs Myers, the pioneers of the Myers Briggs Type Indicator®, observed that individuals prefer either "Thinking" or "Feeling" to some degree when it comes to making decisions.

Individuals with a preference for Thinking typically decide based on impersonal facts and objective logic. The first reaction above is more typical of someone with a Thinking preference.

Individuals with a preference for Feeling typically focus on how a decision will affect people and on values, such as harmony and loyalty. The second reaction above is more typical of someone with a Feeling preference.

Majority of Women "Feel" First

What does this have to do with women and issues of "fit"? *In the general population, it is far more typical for women to have a preference for Feeling—that is, focusing first on how decisions affect people.* In fact, in testing psychological type instruments for validity, researchers found that women are more hesitant to give the "Thinking-preference answer" even when they really think that way, because they feel social pressure to give the "female answer." *While 56% of men show up as having a preference for Thinking, only 25% of women do.*[2]

Vast Majority of Managers "Think" First

The higher one goes in an organization, the higher the likelihood that one's peers have a preference for Thinking. Occupational sample study data shows that 73% of Managers and Administrators[3], 87% of Executives and 90% of Line Managers[4] have a Thinking preference. It can be lonely being a "Feeling" person in a management role. Women who get there are often Thinking types, who approach decision making differently than the majority of women, or Feeling types who learn to consciously and skillfully exercise their Thinking capability as well.

"Feeling" Managers Bring Valuable Benefits

If you're a "Feeling" person feeling lonely at the top of an organization, take heart. You bring a perspective that is highly important and becoming more so in this era:

- Now that so much of the work involving logic, calculation, and analysis can be accomplished through technological means, "people skills" become an even more essential part of human jobs.
- Logic doesn't make things happen. People do. Being able to predict how people will feel and what will likely motivate them can be a big advantage when it comes to getting things done.
- Since the majority—75% of women and 60% of the total population—have a preference for Feeling,[5] it's important to consider strategy and communication from that point of view, as well as a Thinking point of view.
- "Social sensitivity" has been identified by researchers as the strongest single factor in group effectiveness, leading *Humans are Underrated* author Geoff Colvin to conclude that empathy is "the critical 21st-century skill."[6]

Struggles of a "Thinking" Woman

If you're a Thinking-preference executive woman, your natural thinking style—along with your level of responsibility and the experiences you are likely to have had—sets you apart from the general female population. There is often still a subtle expectation that you will behave in a way that is typical for females, even though it's not your most natural approach and it may not be the most suitable approach for your professional role. Others, particularly female colleagues, may be surprised and put off when you jump right on the facts and logic instead of the softer stuff first. It may feel like they have set different standards for you than for your male colleagues. The behavior of a "logical" male colleague who tramples over others without being sensitive to individual needs or feelings may be accepted without much thought, while a much more considerate, but "businesslike," woman may be criticized.

"Flexing" Your Style for Results
The vast majority of managers will expect a logical, analytical approach to decisions, favoring their own Thinking preference. If that's the case and your natural preference is Feeling, be ready to frame your communication in logic so your Thinking manager can hear it.

Conversely, to be more effective with Feeling preference types, a manager—male or female—might consciously work at addressing or acknowledging the "Feeling" side of things—people and values—first with them.

Deliberately considering both the logical and human sides will usually produce better decisions.

"Type Tips" for Smart Managers
Whether your preference is for "Thinking" or "Feeling" first:
- ✓ Know yourself. Become aware of your own style and preferences.
- ✓ Balance your decisions.
  - Consciously consider the decision from both Thinking and Feeling perspectives.
  - Get input from someone who thinks differently from you.
- ✓ To connect most rapidly, consider "flexing" to the other person's preferred style.

Apply & Evaluate: What Do You Notice?
Next time you are faced with a decision, notice:
- *Which tends to be your first reaction—"Thinking" or "Feeling"?*
- *Which is likely to be the first reaction of your boss, colleague, subordinate, or customer?*
- *How might you incorporate both "Thinking" and "Feeling" into your decision making?*

Take Action: Now What?

When making important decisions, consider both "Thinking" and "Feeling" aspects. If you haven't already done so, consider working with a Myers Briggs Type Indicator® professional to learn other ways to access the best from different types on your team.

56 Seven Ways For Women To Come Across More Powerfully At Work

The Challenge: Women Appear Less Confident Than Men at Work

This is not true of all women, certainly, but lack of confidence has been identified as a major factor in women's lagging career progress and compensation. It happens for many reasons.

Women Actually FEEL Less Confident

Even when it's not warranted, women tend to feel less confident at work. Citing several research studies in *The Confidence Code*, Katty Kay and Claire Shipman point out:

- Men tend to overestimate their own performance. Women, on the other hand, tend to underestimate theirs.
- When considering and applying for promotions, women tend to overprepare and hold back, while underqualified and underprepared men tend to be far less hesitant.
- Men are much more likely than women to initiate salary negotiations and ask for more in those negotiations than women.[1]

Male vs. Female Modes: Dominance vs. Equality

Through extensive work on gender dynamics and communication, linguist Deborah Tannen finds a key difference between male and female styles learned outside the workplace.

Men tend to be more comfortable with hierarchy and aim for dominance. Doing so, men go for the "one up" position and avoid the "one down" position.

Women tend to focus more on relationships and are more likely to try to maintain the appearance of equality (especially with other women). As a consequence, women may inadvertently appear less confident and competent.[2]

Women's Communication Rituals Downplay Confidence
To maintain this appearance of equality, women often engage in communication rituals that, at the same time, cause them to appear weaker and less decisive—for instance, apologizing, asking instead of stating, hedging, or making indirect requests instead of giving orders.

Double Standards Work Against Women
Men and women might get totally different reactions when using the same behaviors. Men are expected to speak up in meetings; women who do "talk too much." Male managers are complimented for "taking charge"; female managers are criticized for being "bossy." He's "direct"; she's "abrasive." Men who talk about their families are "balanced"; women who do are "unprofessional." It's not fair, but it still happens. Ironically, women are often their own worst enemies when they are critical of other women or hold greater expectations of them than they do of male colleagues.

The Question: What Can Women Do to Create Stronger Presence?

> **Consider This**
>
> *"Professional success demands political savvy, a certain amount of scheming and jockeying, a flair for self-promotion, and not letting a no stop you. Women often aren't very comfortable with that."*
> —Katty Kay and Claire Shipman, *The Confidence Code*
>
> *"It's time to drop the double standard.*
> *Gender should neither magnify nor excuse rude and dismissive treatment.*
> *We should expect professional behavior, and even kindness, from everyone."*
> —Sheryl Sandberg, *Lean In*
>
> *"I always did something I was a little not ready to do. I think that's how you grow. When there's that moment of 'Wow, I'm not really sure I can do this,' and you push through those moments, that's when you have a breakthrough."*
> —Marissa Mayer
>
> *"You had the power all along, my dear."*
> —Glinda the Good Witch

Try This: Seven Ways Women Can Come Across More Powerfully at Work

1) **Create a More Powerful Physical Presence**
   For better or for worse, most people are influenced first by appearances. Make yours work in your favor:
   - **Dress for how you want to be perceived:** Look the part. Consider wearing darker and stronger plain colors, styles without frills and, perhaps, an appropriate "statement piece" of jewelry to convey more power.
   - **Don't distract:** Keep the focus on your professionalism and message. Don't undermine your professional credibility with revealing clothing or distract from your message with noisy jewelry or fabrics.
   - **Make an entrance:** Enter a room purposefully. Take a deep breath and calmly scan the space. Stand tall with slightly relaxed shoulders.
   - **Watch your face:** Women tend to convey emotions more through facial expressions, while men convey theirs more through body language.[3] Be aware of what your face is saying, as well as your posture and gestures.
   - **Don't over-smile:** Smiling helps create rapport. According to body language experts Allan and Barbara Pease, smiling too much may make women appear subordinate, however. They found that women in business who listen with a more serious face are described by men as more intelligent, astute, and sensible. They suggest that women smile less when dealing with dominant men or mirror the amount of smiling of these men.[4]
   - **Connect eye-to-eye:** Look your audience in the eye. If you are short, try to get closer to the other person's eye level, whether that entails wearing heels, a seated discussion, or a step up behind the podium.
   - **Speak low and project:** Use the lower part of your vocal range. Project your voice by using good posture; by breathing deeply; by keeping your neck, throat, and jaw relaxed; and by pointing it toward the back of the room.
   - **Initiate a handshake:** You'll usually make a better impression and appear more confident if you extend your hand first (except in Muslim cultures) and give a firm handshake.[5]
   - **Keep emotion in check:** In most workplaces, crying and other expression of strong emotion are still not considered acceptable.

In summary, you want to get noticed in a good way!

2) **Speak Up**

In an ideal world, you'd be recognized naturally and fully for your smart ideas and contributions. In the real world, however, you must be willing to speak up.

Women may not get their ideas across successfully or receive deserved credit when 1) they wait to speak up until they feel completely prepared, 2) they get interrupted or don't push back, 3) they downplay their accomplishments, or 4) they don't ask.

Preparation is a key to confidence and effectiveness, so prepare well for meetings and pitches. At the same time, recognize that you may need to speak up without feeling totally prepared. Anticipate issues that may arise. Plan to contribute. Then trust yourself. Sit where you can be seen. Be ready to jump in.

It's likely that you will get interrupted when presenting your ideas. Someone may take over and redirect the conversation. Don't be surprised by this. Have a plan to calmly, but firmly, pull it back if needed.

Keep in mind that when others, and particularly men, state a position as a demand or a given, they may still expect a countermove or challenge. Be ready to tactfully push back if warranted.

Women are often hesitant to brag and turned off by others who do. Men tend to talk more about their own accomplishments. Women tend to de-emphasize their own accomplishments and ask questions that draw out others' accomplishments. If you are fortunate enough to have someone who will "sponsor" you and your ideas, recommend you, and give you credit, that's ideal; most times you will have be prepared to sell yourself. Find a way to comfortably and effectively speak about your accomplishments. Work them into your conversations naturally and smoothly with neither bravado nor apology to make others aware of your talents, experience, and achievements. Use "we" when appropriate, but don't be afraid to use "I" when it's deserved.

Lastly, research shows that women are far less likely than men to ask for more when negotiating salary. Be prepared to make your case and time your request wisely, but do ask.

3) **Be Concise**

Counter to a popular factoid claiming women speak 13,000 more words a day than men, recent research from the Harvard School of Public Health found there's little difference between men and women generally in talkativeness.[6]

Stereotypes of chatty women persist, however, and research shows that women who speak up in meetings may be less liked. For instance, Yale psychologist Victoria L. Brescoli finds that male executives who speak more often than their peers are rated 10% higher on competence, while female executives who do so are rated 14% lower.[7]

Because of this, along with a general attention shortage, you must be concise to be heard. Use fewer, more powerful words. Be strategic. Focus on big issues and results. You can always fill in details and handle issues and questions that arise later.

The Harvard study did find that women speak up more than men in collaborative settings, which gives women an advantage when it's important to gather input, talk things over, and work through details. Deliberately choose this approach when needed. Good collaboration is part of good leadership.

4) **Be Prepared to Defend Your Ideas**
The majority of men and the vast majority of higher-level managers will approach decisions with logic.[8] When evaluating proposals, it's natural for them to focus on impersonal facts and objective standards, while looking for weaknesses and inconsistencies. When they appear critical, it's usually not personal, but rather an attempt to make sure the plan will work. Be ready to calmly and logically defend your ideas.

5) **Limit Rituals That Undermine Your Power**
In *Talking 9 to 5*, Deborah Tannen points out many conversational rituals and "softeners" women use to maintain equality with other women. While these may have a positive effect with some women, they tend to weaken overall effectiveness. Men tend to interpret these as admissions of weakness, fault, or incompetence.

Be aware of these "softeners." Use them purposefully, if at all. For instance:
- **"Ritual Apologies"**: Women often use *"I'm sorry"* as a conversation smoother when they actually have nothing to apologize for, expecting the other person to take half of the blame as part of the ritual. Neither understanding that nor being in that habit, men (and some other women) may take that as an admission of guilt, unnecessarily weakening the woman's position. (A well-delivered authentic apology when warranted, however, is likely to increase effectiveness.)
- **"Ritual Thanks"**: Women often use "thanks" as a conversation closer and a way to maintain the balance with other women. Do

express gratitude when it's deserved, but don't invite others to take undeserved credit.
- **"Upspeak" and Tags**: "Upspeak" is lifting your voice at the end of a sentence as you would when asking a question. Tags are little questions added at the end of sentences, such as *"OK?"*, *"You know?"*, or *"Don't you think?"* Use these, when you are asking for input. Otherwise, drop them, as they make it sound like you are unsure or asking for approval.
- **Fillers, Hedges, and Qualifiers:** Your message will be weakened if you use fillers (*you know, like, um*), hedges (*maybe, try, sort of, perhaps, kind of*) or qualifiers (*This may be a stupid question, I'm not sure, but ...*) to preface your statements. Unless a qualifier is important, plunge right into your statement.
- **Indirect Requests:** Women often ask for what they need through suggestions or indirect requests (*If you could possibly ...*), while men are more likely to give direct orders (*I need this by 5 p.m.*). To get things done, make a diplomatic, direct statement.

6) **Adapt to Your Audience and Culture**
Understand how expectations and rituals vary between men and women; be ready to adapt to your audience. Pay attention, as well, to the values and rituals of your own organization's culture. When presenting, read your audience's body language and adapt accordingly. Watch the response when you make requests; be ready to adjust to be more (or less) direct.

If you feel you're not getting appropriate attention, "airtime," or credit, consider approaching your colleague or leader privately, diplomatically, and in a good-natured way to ask for feedback. If done gracefully, it may increase awareness of any double standard, and you may get some useful advice.

7) **Support Other Strong, Competent Women**
The more higher-level women there are in an organization, the more natural it will be for strong, competent women to feel confident, speak up, be heard, and receive appropriate credit.

In the meantime, within your own team and reach, do what you can to support other deserving women as they strive to get their ideas across, achieve, and progress. When you're leading meetings, interrupt interrupters to let someone finish presenting their ideas. Give proper acknowledgement. Check your own responses to be sure you don't inadvertently judge female colleagues by different standards than you do male colleagues.

Apply & Evaluate: What Do You Notice?
Consider the research on gender differences in the workplace and tips for creating a stronger presence. Pay attention to the dynamics in your workplace and your self-presentation:
- *Do your expectations and reactions differ when dealing with female managers versus male managers? If so, how?*
- *What can you do to achieve a stronger physical presence?*
- *What can you do to communicate your ideas more concisely and confidently? When do you need to speak up earlier or speak up more?*

Take Action: Now What?
Share this research with both female and male colleagues and managers to create a productive dialogue. Awareness of gender differences and dynamics, along with compensating strategies, can be useful to aspiring women. This awareness can also help their managers and colleagues identify ways to bring out their best.

57 Be A Talent Magnet

The Challenge: You're Only as Good as Your Team
As a manager, your overall productivity is a product of the individual and collective productivity of your team members.

The Question: How Can You Attract and Cultivate the Best Talent?
Perhaps the most effective way of attracting a high-quality, high-performing team is to earn a reputation for developing talent. Good people will want to work with you if they feel you will help them progress in their careers.

> "One measure of leadership is the caliber of people who choose to follow you."
> —Dennis A. Peer

Consider This

> "The greatest good you can do for another is not just share your riches,
> but reveal to them their own."
> —Benjamin Disraeli

> "The most significant contribution leaders make is not simply to today's bottom line;
> it is to the long-term development of people and institutions
> so they can adapt, change, prosper, and grow."
> —James M. Kouzes and Barry Z. Posner, *The Leadership Challenge*

> "The conventional definition of management is getting work done through people,
> but real management is developing people through work."
> —Agha Hasan Abedi

Try This: Attract and Develop Talent
Invest time, thought, and energy in your team members' development.

Choose Well
When you hire, in addition to specific job competencies, pay particular attention to the candidate's motivation, fit, and interpersonal skills, as well as how they handle "tough stuff." Are they not only capable, but enthusiastic about their role? Will they get along and collaborate well with their colleagues? Will they take initiative? Will they persist to figure out how to handle difficult challenges?

Get People Off to a Good Start
Give new team members the information, training, connections, and support they need to get off to a good start. The first 90 days or so on the job are critical; some organizations find it beneficial to provide onboarding support for the entire first year. Make new employees feel welcome. Give them a clear picture of your overall purpose and goals. Open doors to make it easy to connect with colleagues. Pair them with peer mentors. Check in at regular intervals. Provide opportunities to ask questions.

Challenge Individuals to Grow
Get to know your team members. Learn about their personal and professional goals, interests, and values. Give individuals assignments that tap into their interests and allow them to use their talents.

Develop Capacities
Give your team members opportunities to further develop their strengths and help them bring critical weaknesses up to standards. Take the time to coach them through challenges. Provide relevant training and education opportunities.

Offer New Experiences
Keep everyone fresh by always providing some type of new experience. Offer assignments that will allow them to apply new skills.

Recognize Achievement
Don't take your talented players for granted. Acknowledge their achievements. Show appreciation for their contributions. Reward them in personally meaningful ways. Consider them first for internal promotions.

Support Individuals' Growth
Make an effort to hold onto talented players. Recognize, though, that at some point, they need to soar. They'll be ready for promotions and further growth; that might mean letting go. It can be hard to let go of good talent, especially if you've invested time and resources in development. If you are letting go to allow someone to progress in their career, consider it a compliment. If you develop a reputation for holding people back selfishly, you are likely to only attract mediocre talent.

Cultivate the Team
Build a culture that supports learning and growth. Promote good collaboration. Encourage team members to support each other's development.

Apply & Evaluate: What Do You Notice?
As you try the above strategies, notice how people respond. Also ask yourself:
- *What do the leaders you know who attract the best talent do that makes them attractive?*
- *If your dream opportunity came along today, could your current role be filled by your existing staff?*
- *Would you want to work on your own team? What else could you do to make your organization one talented people would want to join?*

Take Action: Now What?
As you plan and work toward accomplishing your goals, always keep in mind that your success will largely be because of the talents and efforts of others.

58 Hiring Accountable People

The Challenge: Competence Is Not Enough
Hiring managers usually focus on identifying candidates with relevant knowledge, skills, and experience for their open positions. Such candidates are likely to have what it takes to perform competently; however, sometimes they turn out to be just decent, not great, hires. This can be the case if they don't also engage and put in the thought and energy that drive great performance.

Certainly it's important to consider knowledge, skills, and experience when hiring, but those alone may not be enough. Those answer the question "CAN this person do the job?", but other factors will determine "WILL they do what it takes?" and "Will they thrive?"

The Question: How Can You Identify Candidates Who Will "Make It Happen"?
Along with "fit" and interpersonal skill, one of the key characteristics separating great hires from bad or just adequate ones is their willingness to take initiative and responsibility. The best go beyond routine expectations as they pursue solutions and persist through challenges to "make it happen." There's a difference in the way they look at themselves and the world—a belief that they can make an impact.

If you want your hire to have that "going beyond" mindset, take a good look at their motivation and, specifically, where they fall on the "I Make It Happen" versus "It Happens to Me" continuum.

"I Make It Happen" Behaviors
The person who believes "I Make It Happen" will take charge. Not only will they meet basic job expectations, they are also likely to expend more effort and persist longer as they initiate plans, tackle problems, explore alternatives, create opportunities, negotiate solutions, and act to "do what it takes."

"It Happens to Me" Behaviors

The person who largely believes "It Happens to Me" is likely to behave differently on the job. They're more likely to accept things as they are, "go with the flow," and back off. They'll give up sooner and place more limitations on themselves and others. It wouldn't be surprising to hear them blame, whine, or complain.

Which one do you want?

> **Consider This:**
>
> *"When I'm hiring someone I look for magic and a spark. Little things that intuitively give me a gut feeling that this person will go to the ends of the earth to accomplish the task at hand."*
> —Tommy Mottola
>
> *"Do not hire a man who does your work for money, but him who does it for the love of it."*
> —Henry David Thoreau
>
> *"Hire character. Train skill."*
> —Peter Schutz

Try This: Interview to Uncover Motivation

Ask anyone interviewing for a job if they are motivated and you're pretty sure to get an enthusiastic "Yes!" Most interviewees realize "self-motivated" is part of the interview "right answer."

How will you know who really has the motivation you seek? To uncover authentic answers, you'll need to take an indirect route. There's no guarantee that you will really know until they've been on the job awhile. Still, you can increase your odds of success by deliberately building specific types of questions and techniques into your interview. As you conduct the interview, be alert to motivational issues. Listen. Look. Feel.

"Tough Stuff"

One good way of uncovering a candidate's level of motivation is to ask for examples of how they have handled "Tough Stuff"—tough times, difficult problems, mistakes, and failures. Most candidates are able to come up with at least a few examples of good performance under conventional circumstances. How they deal with "Tough Stuff" may reveal more useful information. Ask for multiple examples. Listen to the language the candidate uses in describing how they dealt with each situation. Winning stories, impressive results, and amazing turnarounds may sound good and may be what they think you want to hear. Listen equally closely for the attitude they took; their candor in describing their role, responsibility, and efforts; and their level of persistence and learning when faced with obstacles. Listen for warning signs. Listen for what is said and left unsaid.

Examples of "Tough Stuff" questions:
Tell me about your ...
- ... toughest customer.
- ... most difficult management issue.
- ... most challenging operational problem.
- ... most impossible goals.
- ... worst boss.

Tell me about a time when ...
- ... you couldn't meet your budget.
- ... you had to do more with less.
- ... you lost a big sale or customer.
- ... you made a bad hire.
- ... you made a big mistake.
- ... you failed.

Go for specifics:
- What was the situation?
- What was your role?
- What did you do?
- What obstacles did you encounter?
- How did it turn out?
- What did you take away from that experience?

Listen
Pay particular attention to the language the candidate uses. This is not about having a big vocabulary or using big words or even being articulate (unless that is part of the criteria for the position). Listen for motivation.

"It Happens to Me" Language
Examples of language you might hear from "It Happens to Me" types:
- I can't, I couldn't.
- Variations of "Not my job."
- It was out of my control.

- *It wasn't my fault.*
- *If so-and-so would/wouldn't have done x.*
- *No one would cooperate/listen/do anything about it.*
- Blaming a bad economy, bad boss, organizational problems, or bad luck without effort to take positive action.

"I Make It Happen" Language
"I Make It Happen" types are more likely to use language such as:
- *I can, I did, I will (versus I'll try).*
- *I knew I could make it work.*
- *I wasn't going to give up.*
- *There's always a solution.*
- *X didn't work, so I tried Y.*
- *I had to get creative.*
- *I had to be persistent.*
- *I'm still working on it.*

Looking At Actions
Some interviewees will simply be good at interviewing. They will say the right things. They will use language that sounds good. Take a look also at what their actions say.

A person with an "I Make It Happen" orientation is likely to face the same amount of challenges as anyone. In fact, they may face more difficult challenges, because they have already attended to the easier ones. What sets them apart is how they handle the challenges.

Faced with difficult challenges or blocked by problems, you are more likely to see them take action. Specifically, you're more likely to see them:
- Take initiative to solve problems.
- Attempt to solve the problem multiple ways if it doesn't yield easily.
- Persist through challenges.
- Learn from mistakes.

Watch with "a third eye" during the interview process. While you ask normal interview questions, pay attention to underlying motivation issues. While you examine resumes, pay attention to values, interests, and motivation. Watch for warning signs, such as job-hopping, but not progressing; or a pattern of "bad bosses" or "bad situations."

Feel: Do a Gut Check
Finally, do a gut check. If something sounds just amazing—even too good to be true—ask yourself how plausible it is. When in doubt, persist in asking

questions. (For example, for a really huge accomplishment, ask "What was your role?") If something bugs you, pay attention to that. Build related questions into your reference and background checks as well.

Avoid Extremes
Most managers find it is easier to tone down motivation than to "create" it. Taken too far, however, an "I Make It Happen" approach can backfire. Sheer personal confidence, extreme egotism, or overaggressive behaviors can lead to big falls or cause problems for colleagues. As in anything, beware of extremes.

Apply & Evaluate: What Do You Notice?
Next time you are hiring, along with the candidate's knowledge, skills, and experience, notice:
- *How much initiative and responsibility do they take generally?*
- *How interested are they in doing the particular job?*
- *In addition to strong motivation, do they have good judgment, flexibility, and interpersonal skill?*

Take Action: Now What?
When you hire an "I Make it Happen" employee, also keep in mind that, once fully onboard, they usually operate best when given some freedom.

Hiring is an opportunity to upgrade your team's talent and performance. Make it great!

59 Collaborative Teams: How To Make 2+2=5

The Challenge: Teamwork Is Not Optional
You can't do it all yourself.

The Question: How Can We Create a Team That Is Greater Than the Sum of Its Parts?
Too often, teamwork adds work and creates further challenges—bureaucracy, politics, miscommunication, distrust. On such teams, 2+2=3, because otherwise-useful energy and skill is spent unproductively.

In contrast, the best teams create energy. Team members encourage, stretch, and inspire each other. They combine ideas and expertise to create a product greater than the sum of the parts.

Consider This

"Everything important in the 21st century will be hyphenated."
—Jerry Allan, Chair, Visual Studies Program,
Minneapolis College of Art and Design

The complex problems of our era, along with increased specialization of knowledge, will require unprecedented collaboration.

"The people who made teams most effective may or may not have been the best knowledge workers. They were definitely the best relationship workers."
—Geoff Colvin

Try This: Create a Consciously-Collaborative Team

As in good marriages, good collaboration sometimes just happens in a good match. When partners are committed to each other, they work things out. Even so, it usually takes conscious attention to everyday communication, processes, and dynamics to achieve the ideal partnership.

Keep the importance of good collaboration in mind when you set up your team, create a culture, and design work processes.

Set Up for Success

Choose team members not only for their technical skills, but for their commitment to your common purpose, collaborative mindset, and interpersonal skill.

Designate roles that capitalize on individual collaborators' strengths, experience, interests, and diverse styles.

Invest time upfront to define your problem or project and desired outcomes. Make sure everyone understands and is committed to those. Additionally, make sure each team member understands how his or her individual responsibilities and goals contribute to your overall mission. Maintain focus on the collective endgame as you define individual goals.

Define a few key metrics to evaluate team performance. Keep them visible so everyone knows how the team is doing. Design your reward system to align with them.

Provide resources team members need to get the job done—connections, information, budget, tools, and time.

Cultivate Collaborative Connections

Know your collaborative partners—not just what their expertise is, but also what they value and how they do their best work. Connect on a personal level first. Discover strengths, experience, values, and interests. Identify what each person needs to be successful.

Promote Trust

Everything flows more easily when team members trust each other. Encourage openness. Make it safe to ask questions. Model constructive ways of expressing thoughts and feelings. Follow through. Walk your talk. Respectfully hold each other accountable.

Prioritize team priorities so if individuals' priorities conflict, they know what's most important. Reward, instead of punish, those who are willing to sacrifice their individual wants for the greater good.

Communication Is the Core of Good Collaboration

Adopt communication practices that support successful collaboration. Share information. Identify different types of stakeholders for your project and involve them as appropriate. Seek input. Acknowledge other perspectives. Ask skillful questions. Listen to each other. If you're stuck, have a dialogue instead of a debate.

Think through communication flow, aiming for productivity: *Who needs information? What's the best way to communicate? When are meetings needed? When is confidentiality required? What response times are expected under normal circumstances? What's your criteria for "urgent" and what's expected then?*

If technology will be useful in your collaborative process, identify the type of technology that works best for your purpose; use it as your servant, not your master.

Even better, encourage face-to-face communication. Create an environment where it's easy for team members to interact informally.

Develop Collaborative Processes

Work out additional processes to streamline and simplify your work and collaboration:

- **Making Decisions:** Outline processes to streamline decisions that come up frequently. Identify team members' roles in each. *Who is responsible? Whose approval is needed? Whose input is needed? Who needs information about the decision?*
- **Managing Resources:** *What resources are needed and how will they be allocated?*
- **Handling Conflict:** *How will disagreements be addressed? How will you handle competing priorities or goals?*
- **Evaluating Performance and Progress:** *How will you measure, report, and evaluate performance? How will you recognize and reward success?*
- **Negotiating Change:** *How will you know when changes are needed? How will you go about it?*

Investing time upfront to outline effective and efficient processes will preserve time and energy in the long-run. From time to time, evaluate how they are working and adjust accordingly.

Grow Together

Successful collaboration often requires patience and adjustment as collaborators develop trust and processes. As Bruce Tuckman discovered, teams go through predictable stages—Forming, Storming, Norming, Performing—as they learn to work together effectively.[1] Learn ways to give respectful and honest feedback. Hold each other accountable. Refine your processes. Acknowledge and celebrate your wins.

Apply & Evaluate: What Do You Notice?
To cultivate a greater-than-the-sum-of-the-parts team, explore:
- *How can we set ourselves up for good collaboration?*
- *What processes will streamline our operations?*
- *What can we do to promote interaction and trust among team members?*

Take Action: Now What?
Apply these strategies with both larger teams and small work groups to increase your leadership capacity and boost your results.

60 Without This, You Won't Get Much Done

The Challenge: Trust in Organizations
Trust undergirds morale, commitment, and performance in organizations. When there is a high level of trust, people feel confident and free to give their best. Without it, they may limit their commitment and hold back, spending otherwise-productive energy on self-protection.

The Question: How Can You Further Trust Within Your Organization?
When the subject of trust comes up in organizations, a first reaction is often thinking of others who may not seem totally trustworthy. Instead, focus first on what you can do in your own role and relationships to cultivate trust.

Consider This:
"Trust rules your personal credibility ... your ability to get things done ... your team's cohesiveness ... your organization's innovativeness and performance ... your brand image. Trust rules just about everything you do."
—James M. Kouzes and Barry Z. Posner, *The Truth About Leadership*

Try This: Identify and Strengthen Trust Behaviors
Trust in organizations begins with trust between individuals.

Trust Is In the Eye of the Beholder

Another's level of trust in you is likely to be a function of the degree to which they believe you are credible, or "CRED":

- **Competent:** You can do what you commit to do.
- **Reasonable:** You're sensible and fair. You have sound judgment.
- **Ethical:** You behave honestly and consider their interests as well as your own.
- **Dependable:** You will deliver on your commitments. There won't be any bad surprises.

Increase Your Trust, Increase Your Influence

To increase your influence in an organization, begin by increasing the trust others have in you.

Start with your own trustworthiness. First, using the following self-assessment, consider your intentions and behavior from your own standpoint. Then go back and pretend you are a specific individual with whom you would like to increase trust. How would they be likely to rate you on these behaviors?

Trust Behaviors: Self-Assessment

Rate yourself on the following behaviors that engender trust between individuals:

We Tend To Trust Someone Who:	Rate Yourself (1–5, 5 Highest)	How Would Another Rate You?
Tells the truth		
Keeps their word		
"Walks their talk"		
Promises only what they can deliver		
Is fair and consistent		
Is competent in the area in which we are associating with them		
Gives appropriate credit to others		

We Tend To Trust Someone Who:	Rate Yourself (1–5, 5 Highest)	How Would Another Rate You?
Admits mistakes and accepts the consequences		
Tells us directly, not others, when we are doing something wrong		
Discloses their agenda and interests		
Defines expectations and communicates clearly		
Alerts us to risks that may affect us		
Seeks to understand others' viewpoints		
Considers our needs and interests as well as their own		
Shares important information and involves us in important decisions that affect us		
Doesn't surprise us with bad news or unpredictable behavior		
Influences us to act in ways that will make us successful		
Uses open body language		
Doesn't abandon us or their principles when times get tough		

Choose 1–3 behaviors from the above list to improve.

Whom Can You Trust?

Trust goes two ways. As you work to both increase the trust others have in you and to determine whom you can trust, keep in mind the following:

- **Trust is earned**: Trust develops over time based on what we experience. If trust is violated, it takes time and effort to rebuild.
- **Trust isn't all or none.** You can trust someone in one role or circumstance, but not in another. You might trust someone in an organization, for instance, with an assignment, but not trust them with personal information.
- **Trustworthiness is more likely under certain conditions**: In her book *Trust Rules*, Loyola University professor Linda Stroh explains that while trustworthy people always "do the right thing," some who aren't totally trustworthy "change their behavior as their goals change." Therefore, it's wise to use caution until one has enough experience with someone to judge their trustworthiness.

    She points out two circumstances under which it's more likely that someone can be trusted: 1) when you share common goals, and 2) in "strong" situations. For social psychologists, a "strong situation" is one in which, due to social controls or cultural practices, most people would behave a certain way, making it easier to predict another's behavior. For instance, people are more likely to follow rules when they know others are watching.[1]

Trust In Organizations

Organizational trust will increase to the degree that:

- *Roles and responsibilities are clearly defined so people know what to expect of each other.*
- *Goals and rewards are aligned so that individuals and departments fully support each other.*
- *Information is shared openly.*
- *People are held accountable to their commitments and for their actions.*
- *People are involved in decisions that affect them.*
- *During times of change, there is good communication. People know what has changed, why, and what the new expectations are.*
- *People in work groups know each other well and have tools and processes to access the best from each other.*
- *Leaders listen. People feel "heard," whether there is agreement or not.*
- *Mistakes or risks are accepted if associated actions were planned and carried out responsibly and if learning takes place.*

Apply & Evaluate: What Do You Notice?
Review the list of trust behaviors and reflect on your workplace relationships:
- *How might your own rating on trust behaviors differ from your colleagues' rating of you?*
- *What actions can you take to earn greater trust?*
- *Who has earned your complete trust? Why?*

Take Action: Now What?
Besides practicing good trust behaviors yourself, consider ways you as a leader can lead, manage, organize, make decisions, communicate, and evaluate and reward performance in ways that will increase trust throughout your organization.

61. Don't Clog The Pipeline: Streamline Decisions

The Challenge: In an Increasingly Fast World, You're Moving Too Slowly

Technology has raised expectations and increased the pace of almost everything. At the same time, organizations are flatter; managers have more on their plates and more direct reports. The need for speed is often in conflict with increased complexity. Routine decisions can be made by computers; we're left with the ones that require human judgment.

The Question: How Can You Make Decisions Faster?

> **Consider This**
>
> *"A good plan violently executed now is better than a perfect plan executed next week."*
> —George S. Patton
>
> *"An expert is someone who has succeeded in making decisions and judgments simpler through knowing what to pay attention to and what to ignore."*
> —Edward de Bono
>
> *"Ever notice that 'what the hell' is always the right decision?"*
> —Marilyn Monroe

Try This: Streamline Decision-Making Processes

Save time and prevent frustration by making processes clear for the types of decisions that come up regularly within your group. For instance, decisions might need to be made regularly related to hiring, spending, policies, or deal structures. For each type of decision, determine the Players and the Process.

Players and Process

Who needs to be involved? What specific role will each party play? For instance, will they:
- Make the decision?
- Approve recommendations?
- Set criteria?
- Provide input?
- Be informed?

Your process options, then, might be:
- **My Decision:** I'll decide by myself.
- **My Decision With Your Input:** I'll consider your input and then I'll decide.
- **Our Decision:** Bring your ideas and we'll decide jointly.
- **My Initial Decision/Your Decision For Further Implementation:** I will decide on and outline major criteria. You make any further decisions that fall within guidelines, along with decisions on details of implementation.
- **Your Recommendation/My Approval:** Bring your recommendation for my approval.
- **Your Decision/I Want To Be Informed Afterward:** Decide and let me know what you did.
- **Your Decision/I Don't Need To Know:** Just decide. I don't need to know about it.
- **We'll Decide How To Handle It If/When It Comes Up:** In unusual situations, we'll decide how to decide on a case-by-case basis.

Make It As Simple As Possible

Think twice before requiring a lot of approvals or imposing too many rules. As Albert Einstein suggested, "Everything should be as simple as possible, but no simpler."

Generally, things will move faster if fewer people are involved in the actual deciding part. That doesn't preclude you from obtaining input from multiple parties before deciding or from explaining your thought process afterward.

Process, Criteria and Timing

For some types of decisions, you'll want to be very specific: *How will the process flow? Will a particular model or tool be used? What criteria will be used to decide? Does it need to fit within certain financial or other bounds? What is the expected turnaround time for approvals?*

Simplify or Specify? Consider Experience and Motivation

Generally, the more experienced the people involved, the less you need to specify. Successful, experienced team members will appreciate your trust and the freedom to do things their way. They'll usually find it more motivating to be trusted with a whole project than just a piece of it.

Clarity Counts

When a manager and staff members are clear and in sync on expectations of how specific types of regularly-occurring decisions will be handled, work flow is faster and simpler, saving time and eliminating a layer of stress. Players move confidently.

Come up with a plan for your group's decision making using the chart below.
- *What are the major types of decisions needed in your area?*
- *Who needs to be involved in each type of decision? What involvement is required?*

Then discuss it with the parties involved and refine it as needed.

How Will Decisions Be Made?

Decision Type	Roles/Involvement	Criteria & Process

Apply & Evaluate: What Do You Notice?

Try the decision-making processes you have outlined for a while and then step back to see how things are working:
- *Are the players clear on the process and their expected involvement?*
- *How has this affected the speed and quality of decision making?*
- *What adjustments are needed? Could the process be simplified?*

Take Action: Now What?

Review and refine your processes periodically, considering staff members' development and other changes that have occurred.

62 Where To Set Your Challenge Thermostat

The Challenge: Too Much Stress? Too Much Comfort?
At some point, pressure becomes unproductive. People can't do their best when they're exhausted or freaking-out-fearful.

On the other hand, boredom is a dangerous enemy. Too little pressure may result in a different set of detrimental problems.

How's the level of challenge these days for you and your team? Do you need to turn up the heat or cool things off?

The Question: How Do You Set a Productive Balance Between Comfort and Stress?

> **Consider This**
>
> *"Many of us feel stress and get overwhelmed not because we are taking on too much, but because we're taking on too little of what really strengthens us."*
> —Marcus Buckingham
>
> *"Do one thing every day that scares you."*
> —Eleanor Roosevelt
>
> *"Each success only buys an admission ticket to a more difficult problem."*
> —Henry Kissinger

Try This: Find the Most Productive Level of Challenge

Which is Worse—Too Much Comfort or Too Much Stress?
If asked which is better, being too stressed or being too comfortable, most rational people wouldn't have to think twice before choosing comfort. In the

midst of oversized challenge, we may think comfort is the goal. If only we could get some.

Being comfortable is comfortable, but it's not ideal for productivity.

Consequences of Too Much Comfort
Too much comfort brings less obvious dangers than too much stress. It starts as a little relief and then grows into sluggishness. When we're not challenged, we may ease up. Not being alert, we miss crucial warning signs. If we don't have enough meaningful work to do, we may invent busywork and call it important. We may even unwittingly invent drama to fill the boredom. If it took hard work to get to a place of comfort, we may still believe we are working hard. We may "rest on our laurels." A sense of entitlement may creep in. When we are too comfortable, we resist change. We avoid taking risks. We don't recognize that what made us successful in the past may not be enough for future success.

Too Much Comfort?
If your team is a little too comfortable, consider the following strategies:
- **Set the bar a notch higher.** Require a little more. Then nudge the bar up again. You might run into resistance. (*Oh, we couldn't possibly do more. We're already so busy.*) Be both fair and firm. If you find your assumptions are wrong about more being possible, you can readjust, but start by increasing the level of challenge.
- **Hold people accountable.** Be clear on expected outcomes. Measure performance. Establish consequences. Reward good performance visibly. Actively coach those who could be contributing more. Fire a chronic non-performer. While most of us dread firing anyone, showing that slacking doesn't cut it is likely to have a dramatic positive effect on the motivation of good performers when they see their efforts aren't for naught.
- **Shake things up.** Give people something new to do. Throw out a big challenge. Redefine roles and responsibilities. Bring in some "fresh eyes" to question the status quo. Reward strategic risk taking.
- **Create a sense of urgency.** Dramatize the need for change or improvement with a visible example. Make it one in which people can recognize consequences for themselves—both the risks of staying stuck and the benefits of pushing themselves to a higher level. Focus on what's needed for success in the future.

Serious Stress and Freakin' Fear

At the other end of the continuum, too much can just be too much. Too much pressure may cause unproductive stress. Not only is excessive stress often associated with health problems, productivity may be compromised when there is too much fear. When people are too anxious, they may freeze or take on unproductive behaviors to try to protect themselves. For instance, under pressure to reach a key goal, they may make ethical compromises or "game the system" in ways that cause other problems. When people feel insecure, they probably won't be able to concentrate fully on the work at hand as they are tempted to spend excessive time and energy on rumors and politics.

Too Much Fear or Stress?

If there's too much fear or stress in your work group, consider the following:

- **Walk around**. Talk with people. Watch how things are actually working. Don't just rely on reports and data.
- **Do the things that count**. Establish clear priorities and expectations. Focus on the highest-impact activities. Consider letting some unimportant things go. Look for ways to simplify, streamline, or hand off activities.
- **Be visible. Be available.** Overcommunicate, especially about priorities. Share information. Listen.
- **Provide resources.** Make sure the needed resources—information, connections, materials, equipment, budget, or training—are available.
- **Acknowledge the importance of good self-care.** If people don't take care of personal needs, such as rest and nutrition, they're unlikely to be in good shape for anything else.
- **Create trust.** Cultivate strong relationships. Model what you want to see from others. Align your words and actions. Reward cooperation.

Stretch, Not Stress

In his book *Finding Flow*, psychologist Mihaly Csikszentmihalyi identifies an ideal state in which one is "in the zone." In this state of "flow," our energy is focused on something meaningful and we're fully engaged. We have a clear set of goals and receive immediate feedback on how well we are doing. Our skills are fully deployed; the challenge is just manageable.

The ideal place to be for best productivity, then, is where you are stretched a bit, but not stressed. You're alert; you're working on something you consider worthwhile. There's an element of challenge; you are learning. The goal is within reach, but you have to work for it.

Apply & Evaluate: What Do You Notice?
Think of times when you and your team were most productive. Then consider:
- *On a scale where 0=no pressure at all and 10=very high pressure, where are you most productive?*
- *Where can you challenge yourselves more?*
- *How will you recognize the signs of too much stress? When you see that, what adjustments could you make, at least for a time?*

Take Action: Now What?
One way to achieve a productive balance between comfort and stress is to always have some element of your work that is new, as well as something that is familiar. Aim for at least 25% of your work to involve something new each year —for example, taking on new clients, new territory, new projects, using new skills, or looking at new types of problems.

63 Tailored Delegation

The Challenge: You Don't Want to Micromanage, But …

Even if you wanted to, you probably don't have time to micromanage. The average number of direct reports per manager has increased over the last two decades, while the pace has quickened.[1]

At the same time, more complex problems in many fields require greater specialization and collaboration. Rapid change requires more frequent communication and adjustments.

The Question: How Can You Maintain Control of Delegated Projects Without Interfering?

> **Consider This**
>
> *"Few things help an individual more than to place responsibility upon him, and to let him know you trust him."*
> —Booker T. Washington

Try This: Tailored Delegation

Don't Do "The Delegation Dump"!

You've heard people complain about their micromanaging bosses, so you've vowed you'll never be one of those. You hand the whole project over and head to the gym. Yes! It's off your plate now. The day the assignment is due you seek out the guy you gave it to and—guess what? It's not done or it's done poorly; or it's done, but not in the way you intended; or things have changed since you handed it off.

Micromanagement is not good delegation, but neither is dumping and running. There may be times when handing a project over in its entirety and bowing out is appropriate, but often some ongoing communication and management is beneficial. After all, even if the project is delegated, as a manager, you are still responsible.

Delegating the Dregs
About that project you dumped—it was real work worthy of the other guy's time, right? Sometimes managers just delegate work they don't want to do. Few of us can entirely avoid uninteresting tasks, but nobody wants to only receive others' castoffs. Before you hand off those dregs, make sure it's work worthy of being done at all!

Are You Hovering?
For many workers, the only thing worse than a boss who "dumps" is one who hovers. While hoverers usually have very good intentions, from the experienced staffer's seat it looks like their manager doesn't trust them. They'd prefer the freedom to carry out the assignment their way.

When Delegating, One Size Doesn't Fit All
The optimal amount of involvement largely depends on two factors: 1) the experience of the person to whom you're delegating, and 2) the importance, complexity, and risk involved in the project. A more experienced staffer generally requires less direction and manager involvement, while a less experienced person will likely appreciate more support. The more important, complex, or risky the project, the more it may also warrant continuing involvement. Fortunately, there are many involvement options between hovering and dumping.

The Delegation Conversation
Effective delegation begins with choosing the right person for the assignment and conducting a clear delegation conversation including:
- The purpose of the project
- Why it is important
- Why they were chosen to do it
- What success will look like
- How their work will be evaluated
- Timeframe
- Resources
- Boundaries
- Your expected involvement and follow-up plan

The person to whom you are delegating may also need:
- An opportunity to ask questions immediately; or an opportunity to think about it or work with it and then ask questions.
- Access to you, to others, to resources, and to information.
- Support, feedback, and checkpoints along the way to assess progress and make refinements if needed.

The Follow-Up Plan
Build a follow-up plan fitting the assignment and the experience level of the delegatee into your delegation strategy:
- Determine how you will receive information and track progress, such as in interim meetings or through progress reports. Require only information you will use.
- Determine an appropriate process to answer questions, address changes, troubleshoot developments, and provide additional input along the way, if needed.
- Don't intervene otherwise unless it's really necessary. If you do, provide an explanation.
- Don't take back delegated responsibility and decision making. Provide clarification, information, and support, if needed, but maintain the roles and responsibilities as delegator and delegatee unless there is some critical reason to change.

Reducing Risk
If you're concerned about risk involved in a delegated project, consider these risk-reducing strategies:
- Break the project up into smaller pieces.
- Shorten the timeframe to allow time for fixes if needed or ...
- Lengthen the timeframe to give more time for learning.
- Adjust the delegatee's other responsibilities to allow them to devote greater focus, time, and energy to the project.
- Consider additional resources.

Learning In Progress
When the delegatee is learning new skills or processes:
- Establish checkpoints along the way.
- Balance freedom and control.
- Acknowledge learning and progress.
- Where there are concerns, give feedback, work together to generate alternatives, and agree on next steps.

In a Crunch?
If it's not important, consider relaxing your standards. Focus on the required outcome.

Apply & Evaluate: What Do You Notice?
Next time you are delegating a project, ask yourself:
- *Does the person I'm delegating this to have a clear understanding of the assignment—why they are doing it, what a successful outcome will look like, and our respective roles?*
- *Do they have the time and resources to get it done?*
- *Do we have a follow-up plan that will keep it on track?*

Take Action: Now What?
Tailor your delegation conversations and plans to fit the project and person to whom you are delegating. To the extent possible, delegate to someone with good motivation to do the job. Choose someone whose strengths and interests match the opportunity. A little stretch is good for learning and engagement. Give them as much freedom as possible to do it their way.

64. Are You Dreading Performance Reviews?

The Challenge: The Dreaded Annual Performance Review
If you dread performance reviews, you're not alone. Most people do—both managers and their employees. They grit their teeth and force their way through a required form to get it over with, often at the last minute, to comply with their organizations' requirements.

The Question: How Can You Increase the Usefulness of Performance Conversations?

> **Consider This**
>
> *"The bad news is that ignoring the performance of people is almost as bad as shredding their effort in front of their eyes. ... The good news is that by simply looking at something that somebody has done, scanning it, and saying 'uh huh,' [you] dramatically improve people's motivations."*
> —Dan Ariely[1]

Try This: Regular, Constructive, Collaborative Performance Conversations
The evolution of the business environment calls for a simultaneous evolution of the "performance planning" process. The faster pace of business, broader reach of managers, greater demands on employees, and sweeping consequences of change call for more frequent, focused communication.

While the process catches up, most managers still have to fill out the official annual forms. Here are some ways to improve the required annual process, while supplementing it with practices that promote optimal performance and growth throughout the year.

Think Bigger

Consider the potential value of performance conversations beyond the paperwork as an opportunity for the employee and manager to simply have each other's uninterrupted, full attention to explore important issues that get lost in the flurry of day-to-day activity. For instance, it can be a time to:

- Clarify expectations and address concerns.
- Collaborate to boost performance.
- Address obstacles.
- Express appreciation.
- Acknowledge potential and share aspirations.
- Scan the horizon to anticipate change, opportunities, or risks.
- Create new goals.

Regular Check-ins

If you're not already doing so, set up regular briefer "check-ins" during the year—monthly one-on-one meetings, for instance—or even very brief weekly meetings. These meetings allow you to ensure that progress is being made, anticipate problems, make needed shifts, address obstacles, and acknowledge and build on successes. (As you do this, collect examples of achievements and demonstrated competencies so they'll be handy when you have to prepare formal assessments later.) Consistently coach for improvement.

Check-in meetings need not be long or paper-heavy. Don't skip them, though. This discipline will maintain momentum, support development, prevent surprises, allow you to capitalize on timely opportunities, and keep everyone focused.

Constructive Conversations

Make conversations constructive by focusing on:

- **What's Controllable:** *What can you control, change, or influence?*
- **The Future:** *What can you do moving forward?*
- **What's Most Important:** *What are your highest priorities at this time and how can you make an impact on them?*
- **Actions and Behaviors:** *What actions can you take to drive your desired results? What behaviors will increase effectiveness?*
- **Learning:** *What have you learned that will help or change things in the future?*

Use facts when appropriate, but don't disregard feelings. Use "I" statements to express opinions, feelings, suggestions, and needs: *From my perspective ... , This is how it appears to me. I felt this. I hoped for that. I need x. I could do y.*

Collaborative Conversations

A meeting in which both parties are engaged and contributing to the conversation is bound to be much more motivating and useful than an "I talk, you listen" meeting. Set up your meetings as two-way conversations where both parties provide input and participate in solution-finding.

In work that involves more than one person, the output depends not just on the individual expertise and effort of each, but also on their effectiveness in working together. Pause from time to time to assess how your work process is going. What would help you be more productive? Share perspectives one at a time. Listen carefully to each other and ask for clarification if needed, without disputing or defending your position. Aim to see the other person's point of view. Then discuss: *What, if any, changes should we make that would improve our collaboration? What can we do to improve overall results?*

Coaching Conversations

Regular check-in meetings also provide an opportunity for coaching and development. Skills and capacities are developed over time with focus, learning, practice, and feedback. The meetings themselves also provide an opportunity to hone important skills, such as self-evaluation, collaboration, communication, strategic thinking, and problem-solving.

Three Ways to Make the Formal Performance Review More Useful

Regular check-ins will keep you from spending your more strategic midyear and year-end meetings handling the latest crises. Increase the value of your formal reviews three ways:

1) **Connect the Dots**

    In most organizations, the performance review "rating" and paperwork are used as input for determining salary increases. Along with that, think of formal midyear and annual reviews in the greater context of strategic performance management.

    Use your preparation time and discussion to move forward on other parts of this process, such as **goal setting** for the next year, **resource allocation**, and **talent development**. It's a time to address larger career issues by identifying strengths and growth opportunities, discussing aspirations, and exploring potential career paths. The thinking and focus involved in both the manager's and employee's preparation, along with dialogue in the review meeting, can also lead to **new ideas, adjustments, and improvements.**

2) **Two-Way Preparation**

To make your meeting time most productive, ask the employee to prepare to discuss their own performance, needs, and forward-looking recommendations. For instance, you might ask them to be prepared with:

Self-Evaluation

Evaluate your own performance:
- *How does your performance compare to the goals set? How does it compare to the organization's standards?*
- *What do you consider your major accomplishments? What do you feel you did particularly well? What has improved during the period?*
- *Which goals, if any, were not accomplished? Why? Are these still appropriate goals? If so, what would need to happen for the goal to be met?*

Input for Goals

Consider goals for the next period:
- *What changes have occurred or are anticipated—in the field, in the organization, or for individuals? Given these, what, if any, changes are appropriate to our focus and goals going forward?*
- *What new opportunities exist?*
- *What does success look like and how will we measure it?*

Needs and Resources

Consider what you need to maximize performance:
- *What do you need from your manager?*
- *What resources are needed?*

Development

Consider your own development:
- *What are your career goals?*
- *Which strengths would you like to further cultivate? Which skills do you feel you'd like to or need to develop?*
- *What do you think would be the best way to pursue that learning?*

3) **Make It Meaningful**
   Forms used for formal performance reviews have often been created to apply to a broad range of jobs and levels. Consider ways you can meet the formal requirements of your organization, while making the process more pertinent to your own department. For instance, note and focus on the critical success factors and skills for your particular roles.

Apply & Evaluate: What Do You Notice?

Evaluate your current performance management process and identify ways to make it more productive:
- *How can you use regular check-ins to improve reaction time, skills, and results?*
- *How can you improve the usefulness of formal midyear and annual performance reviews?*
- *What can you do to make your performance conversations more constructive and collaborative?*

Take Action: Now What?

Apply the same principles to your own performance reviews and conversations with your superior. Take the initiative to self-evaluate and prepare in advance. In addition to required formal performance reviews, aim for shorter, more frequent performance conversations.

65 Update Your Motivation Methods

The Challenge: Staying Engaged
According to research conducted regularly by the Gallup Organization, only 32% of Americans are "engaged" at work. These "engaged" workers are the ones who really care about their jobs and organization and put in discretionary effort. The majority, 51%, are "disengaged," just putting in their time, while 17% are "actively disengaged" and may be doing actual damage by spreading their negativity.[1] While the exact numbers vary slightly from month to month and across countries, the pattern is consistent. The majority of workers don't feel like giving their all—and it's not just lower-paid workers who feel that way.

What a shame. All that wasted time and human energy! What if you could flip those numbers so that the majority were "engaged"?

How about you? Be honest. Are you "engaged" at work? Given current economic forecasts and life expectancy, you're likely to be working a long time.

The Question: How Can You Stay (and Keep Others) Motivated?
The world of work has changed and continues to change in many ways. Most of us are operating in a more competitive global arena. Job security can't be assumed.

The nature of human work is evolving, too. Technology has freed us from much drudgery, while making some jobs and professions obsolete. With computers, robots, and software taking care of more routine tasks and standard scenarios, our remaining work will be more challenging and also potentially more fulfilling.

Our thinking about motivation must evolve to match the challenges and opportunities of our new work world.

> **Consider This**
>
> *"People will be most creative when they feel motivated primarily by the interest, satisfaction, and challenge of the work itself—and not by external pressures."*
> —Teresa Amabile[2]
>
> *"Purpose provides activation energy for living. I think that evolution has had a hand in selecting people who had a sense of doing something beyond themselves."*
> —Mihaly Csikszentmihalyi

Try This: Update Your Motivation Methods

We Can't "Motivate" Each Other

Motivation is defined as "the general desire or willingness of someone to do something." It's seen in enthusiasm, "get up and go," determination, and drive. Motivation is that spark that impels the quantity and quality of our work, as well as our willingness to persist through the tough stuff.

In the short-term, others might "move" us by force, persuasion, or incentives, but in the long-run, it's largely up to us. Someone else might force you to do something, but they can't make you do it with enthusiasm and determination. Others can't really motivate us; they can only tap into our motivation.

Motivation Is Individual

What moves a person varies dramatically from individual to individual, depending on what they value most. One who values wealth most, for instance, would "move" quite differently than one who values security or community or harmony most.

Traditional External "Motivators" Only Go So Far

Traditional workplace motivators have largely been external "carrots and sticks"—salary, benefits, incentives, awards and rewards, policies, penalties, or punishments—ways managers tried to move and satisfy workers by pushing and pulling from the outside.

External motivators can be important, but they only go so far. Most workers would agree that compensation is very important, although for many, other things may mean more than additional financial rewards at a certain point.

Another problem with external motivators is that, once in place, it's hard to withdraw them. Take away an incentive or commission program and watch what happens. A few people will continue to perform at a high level; those top performers probably did so before you put the incentive plan in place.

Twenty-first Century Work Requires Internal Motivation
In *Drive: The Surprising Truth About What Motivates Us*, Daniel Pink points out that changes in work change the motivation game, as well. With routine work, a "carrot" or "stick" might move a worker to work faster. Twenty-first century work, however, increasingly involves creativity, judgment, thinking, collaboration, and interpersonal savvy. These can't be forced from the outside. The impetus must come from within.[3]

Harvard professor and creativity expert Teresa Amabile finds, "The desire to do something because you find it deeply satisfying and personally challenging inspires the highest levels of creativity, whether it's in the arts, sciences, or business."[4]

Likewise, true service orientation can't be forced. While you can set up standards, procedures, and incentives, you can't make someone be nice to others or care about them.

For many types of "Twenty-first Century Work," motivation from the inside becomes vital. Tap into this internal motivation three ways: Flow, Fit, and Freedom.

Flow
Have you ever been working at something so intently that you lost sense of time or even lost sense of self? Mihaly Csikszentmihalyi calls this state of complete focus "flow." It's the ultimate "engagement."

According to Csikszentmihalyi, certain conditions are needed for "flow" to occur:
- You're doing something **active.**
- It's very **interesting.**
- It provides the right amount of **challenge**. It's "just about manageable"—you have to be alert and you are stretched a little, but not overwhelmed.
- You get immediate **feedback** so you know how you're doing.[5]

Fit
Think of people you know who have sacrificed for their work. What makes them do so? Their work is probably a great "fit" for them in at least one of several ways:
- **Values:** It provides an opportunity for them to pursue a cherished personal value—achievement, service, prestige, justice, wisdom, order, or beauty, for instance.

- **Interests:** It's a compelling fit with their interests. They're driven to discover or express something. For them, the "work is more fun than fun," as Noel Coward put it. (This doesn't mean it's without challenge or conflict.)
- **Purpose:** It's directly related to what they see as their life mission.
- **Suitability and Style:** It's a fit with who they are. For instance, they have a natural service-orientation or creative drive.
- **Meaning:** It's deeply meaningful in some way.

As writer John Irving described it, *"The unspoken factor is love. The reason I can work so hard at my writing is that it's not work for me."*

Freedom

Self-determination can be motivating in several ways. We're usually a lot more committed to goals we set for ourselves and when we have a say in things that affect us. Innovative companies such as Google and 3M are known for letting staffers dedicate a portion of their time to work on projects of their own choosing. Companies such as Best Buy and the Gap have experimented with ROWE™, a Results-Only Work Environment, in which workers can determine when and how they do their work, as long as they produce the desired results.[6]

Being able to choose our work, to control how we use our time, and to do the work our way can make a big difference in our on-the-job engagement.

Pursue Flow, Fit, and Freedom both in your own career planning and in managing and leading others.

It's Up to You

It's largely up to you to motivate yourself at work. Look for work that truly interests you. Find an environment that allows you to do your best work. Keep challenging yourself. If you find you're forcing yourself or dragging, consider a change.

Tips for Managers

While you can't force others to be "motivated," there are several ways you can increase the likelihood of having an "engaged" staff:

1) **Hire For Fit and Motivation**
   Be alert to motivational issues when you hire and assign work. Hire self-motivated people with genuine interest in the work. Along with skills and experience, look for a good match between the candidate's passion and style and your work and workplace. Recognize individuals' values,

interests, strengths, and preferences when you determine work responsibilities and assignments.

2) **Provide the Right Amount of Challenge**
Set worthy goals—ones that are neither too easy nor impossible. Provide opportunities to stretch and grow. We do best when we're aspiring and learning.

3) **Give as Much Freedom as Possible Within the Work**
Be sure your team understands their overall purpose and goals, along with their expected roles and results; then, give them as much freedom as possible to do the work their way.

When possible, assign an entire project, instead of just a small piece of it, so team members can be responsible for and see the results of their work.

4) **Balance External and Internal Rewards**
Recognize the importance of internal motivation and personal satisfaction for the long-haul and for complex or creative work. Recognize, as well, when external rewards will be effective in focusing short-term attention, for fulfilling basic needs, and for reinforcing the internal rewards in tangible ways.

Apply & Evaluate: What Do You Notice?
Think about what really "moves" you and your team members:
- *How can you tap into individuals' (including your own!) internal motivation?*
- *When would an external reward, such as a short-term incentive or award, provide a boost?*
- *How can you provide team members freedom and choices?*

Take Action: Now What?
Keep motivational issues clearly in mind when you hire, assign work, and design your work processes and rewards.

66 Put Humor To Work

The Challenge: Work's Become a Drag
You're stuck. You're bored. You're overloaded. You're unproductively replaying the past. You're disengaged. Even the best of us drag at times.

The Question: How Can You Lighten Up, Without Compromising Your Serious Purpose?
No doubt, your mission and responsibilities are serious. Even so, to break out of a funk or enhance your productivity, it may help to treat yourself and your situation with a touch of humor.

> **Consider This**
>
> *"Mix a little foolishness with your prudence: It's good to be silly at the right moment."*
> —Horace

Try This: Put Humor to Work
Humor can provide many benefits in the workplace. It can help:
- Attract and hold attention.
- Build rapport.
- Counter stress.
- Smooth difficult conversations.
- Bring unexpected solutions to light.

Humor: What Works At Work
Lighten up and enhance your work atmosphere by using humor five ways:

1) **Begin With a Grin**

   Joy is attractive. I've only met a few people in my life who didn't love to laugh.

   Speakers often draw listeners in by beginning with a joke or humorous story. An effective one will increase your likability. Make sure it's relevant to your audience and topic. Practice your delivery until it's smooth.

   Not only will you capture attention by using humor, you and your message will be more memorable. Media researchers have found that humorous ads are more involving and enjoyable, making them more memorable and impactful.[1] A study by Sam Houston State University psychologist Randy Garner finds that students are more likely to recall a statistics lecture when relevant jokes are interjected.[2]

   You might be surprised to learn that a little humor during the interview process can give you an advantage, as well. In a study of more than 2,000 hiring managers and human resources professionals conducted by Harris Interactive©, employers were asked which factors would make them consider one equally-qualified candidate over another; a better sense of humor was a top factor.[3] While you certainly need to convey your serious interest in and suitability for the position, consider adding a dash of humor.

   Once you're hired, skillful use of humor can also give you an edge. According to Fabio Sala's research, executives ranked as "outstanding" used humor more than twice as often as "average" executives.[4]

2) **Create a Connection**

   > *"Laughter is the shortest distance between two people."*
   > —Victor Borge

   Humor can provide a quick way to establish rapport by hinting at what we have, or experience, in common. In difficult negotiations or stressful situations, it can break the tension. When there's a big difference in age, professional level, or experience, leaders may find self-deprecating humor helps put others at ease by showing they're human, too.

3) **Provide Comic Relief**

   > *"Laughter is an instant vacation."*
   > —Milton Berle

   Researchers have determined that humor is good for our health. According to the Mayo Clinic, laughter not only lightens your mental load, but induces positive physical changes in your body. It enhances your oxygen intake, stimulating your heart, lungs, and muscles. It increases the release of feel-good endorphins and reduces stress symptoms. Longer term, it may also improve your immune system and relieve pain.[5]

So let go. Have a good laugh.

4) **Tell the Truth**

"My way of joking is to tell the truth. It's the funniest joke in the world."

—G. B. Shaw

Some humor is funny because it is so true. We can allow ourselves to laugh at someone else's parallel predicament. When the truth hurts, humor can be used to point it out indirectly and diplomatically. A touch of humor can smooth the way when we need to communicate difficult messages or tactfully disagree.

5) **Shift Your Mindset**

When in the midst of difficult problems, a friend of mine often suggests, "Sometimes you've just got to go to the movies." When you're stuck, sluggish, or down, shifting your focus to something funny can raise your spirits and help you see things differently. Research by neuroscientist Karuna Subramaniam confirms that putting people in a lighter mood increases their likelihood of experiencing "Eureka!" moments and greater inspiration.[6] You're likely to have a more fruitful brainstorming session if you begin by showing some comic clips.

Don't Bomb: What's Not Funny

Well-timed, well-delivered humor can lighten the atmosphere, create bonds between individuals, and open up thinking. Inappropriate, ill-timed, or poorly delivered humor, however, can poison the atmosphere, cause hurt feelings and misunderstandings, undermine trust, or shut down creativity.

For best results, keep the following points in mind when adding humor to your workplace:

Consider Your Role

Before you crack that joke, consider whether it will help or hurt your credibility and effectiveness.

Leaders are often well-received when they make fun of themselves, because they are seen as more human and approachable. Linguist

Deborah Tannen's research suggests, however, that this may work better for men than for women. Because men commonly engage in ritual "razzing" of each other to put themselves in a "one up" position, when a woman puts herself down, they may be happy to interpret that at face value.[7] Self-deprecating humor works best when the ones putting themselves down clearly have more power. Don't take yourself too seriously, but also be careful what you voice.

Consider the traditional role of The Jester in royal courts. Rulers found it useful to have someone around to lighten the mood or to say things they couldn't say themselves. If you take on this role, you're likely to be popular in the office, but don't overdo it if you also want to be taken seriously.

When you add humor, make sure it's the type that you can carry off. Men sometimes can pull off suggestive humor; women almost never can; and both may suffer damage as a result. Laughter generally increases likability, but nervous laughter may appear as insecurity.

Consider Your Audience
Who is your audience? What's funny to them? What have they been through or what are they going through? Will they have a sense of humor about this? Choose your topics, timing, and tone carefully. What's funny to you may not be to them; individuals may be particularly sensitive to certain subjects.

Consider Your Timing
A well-placed quip is likely to be well-received. A poorly timed one can have devastating consequences. While it's often true that you'll later "look back at this and laugh," your audience may not yet be ready to do that. Before making light of a situation with a witty comment intended to break the tension, consider whether the topic might be too serious to someone else at the moment.

Consider Your Topic and Tone
Generally, it's appropriate to make fun of yourself, but not of others. Even the most confident among us may feel hurt by public ridicule. It's often appropriate to make fun of shared situations, but not another's personal misfortunate.

Avoid sensitive topics and comments that may be misconstrued, offensive, or hurtful. Resist the temptation to throw out that clever "gotcha." It's better not to have to, but be ready to add "I was kidding" if you were and it appears there's any doubt.

Sarcasm is sometimes clever, but often hurtful. Exaggeration can be funny, but mockery stings. Along with alienating others, showing even a little underlying anger, mean-spiritedness, or cynicism may damage your own reputation.

Evaluate & Apply: What Do You Notice?
Consider ways you can use humor effectively in your workplace:
- *Where can you add some levity to raise spirits and results?*
- *In your role, what type of humor works best?*
- *To what type of humor does your audience or team respond best? From which topics is it best to stay away?*

Take Action: Now What?
Increase your comedic capacities by watching comedians and collecting humorous material. Add a little levity to meetings and presentations. Consider additional ways you can add some fun to the workplace.

Humor works. No joke!

APPENDIX

Notes

Learning & Change
Learning to Lead
1. James M. Kouzes and Barry Z. Posner, *The Truth About Leadership* (San Francisco: Jossey-Bass, 2010), 17.

Career Planning for a Technology-Enabled World
1. U.S. Bureau of the Census, U.S. Bureau of Labor Statistics.

Today's #1 Success Skill: Learning
1. Price Pritchett, *Carpe Mañana* (Pritchett Rummler-Brache, 2000), 9.

2. "Mass Use of Inventions," *singularity.com*, www.singularity.com/charts/page50.html.

3. Carl Benedikt Frey and Michael A. Osborne, "The Future of Employment: How Susceptible are Jobs to Computerisation?" *Oxford Martin School*, September 17, 2013, www.oxfordmartin.ox.ac.uk/downloads/academic/The_Future_of_Employment.pdf.

Strategic Productivity
The Truth About Multitasking
1. Debra Viadero, "Instant messaging found to slow students' reading," *Education Week*, August 15, 2008, www.edweek.org/ew/articles/2008/08/27/01im.h28.html.

2. Joshua S. Rubinstein, David E. Meyer, and Jeffrey E. Evans, "Executive control of cognitive processes in task switching," *Journal of Experimental Psychology: Human Perception and Performance* 27, No. 4 (2001), 763-797.

3. Ron Alsop, *The Trophy Kids Grow Up: How the Millennial Generation is Shaking Up the Workplace* (San Francisco: Jossey-Bass, 2008), 154.

4. David Rock, *Your Brain at Work: Strategies For Overcoming Distraction, Regaining Focus and Working Smarter All Day Long* (New York: HarperCollins, 2009), 36.

5. Pat Heim and Susan Murphy, *In the Company of Women: Turning Workplace Conflict into Powerful Alliances* (New York, Tarcher, 2001), 77.

6. Alsop, *The Trophy Kids Grow Up*, 154.

7. Rubinstein, Meyer and Evans, quoted in *Leadership Strategies* 4, No. 12 (December 2001).

Information Overwhelm: The Culling Cure
1. David Shenk, "Why You Feel the Way You Do," *Inc.*, January 1, 1999, www.inc.com/magazine/19990101/708.html.

2. Nicholas Carr, *The Shallows: What the Internet is Doing to Our Brains* (New York: Norton, 2011), 115–116.

Grinding Your Gears? Take a Refresh Break
1. Carmen Nobel, "Reflecting on Work Improves Job Performance," *Harvard Business School Working Knowledge*, May 5, 2014, http://hbswk.hbs.edu/item/7509.html.

Seven Ways to Decide
1. Rushworth Kidder, *How Good People Make Tough Choices: Resolving the Dilemmas of Ethical Living* (New York: Morrow, 1995).

2. Edward de Bono, *De Bono's Thinking Course* (New York: Facts on File, 1994), 12–19.

Beyond SWOT: Five Simple Strategy Models
1. Jackie Stavros, David Cooperrider and Lynn Kelley, "Strategic Inquiry > Appreciative Intent: Inspiration to SOAR," *AI Practitioner* (November 2003).

Creativity & Innovation
Help! I'm Not Creative
1. George Ainsworth-Land and Beth Jarman, *Breakpoint and Beyond: Mastering the Future Today* (New York: HarperCollins, 1992). In a test of divergent thinking, 98% of kindergardeners scored at the genius level; at age 10, 32% scored at that level; at age 15, 10% did. In a test of 200,000 adults over the age of 25, only 2% scored at the genius level.

2. Howard Gardner, *Intelligence Reframed: Multiple Intelligences for the 21st Century* (New York: Basic, 2000).

Ignite Your Creative Capacity
1. Po Bronson and Ashley Merryman, "The Creativity Crisis," *Newsweek*, July 10, 2010, www.newsweek.com/creativity-crisis-74665.

Innovation: It's Not Just About New Products
1. J. J. Colao, "An E-Commerce Giant Reveals Its Strange Strategy: Sending Customers To Competitors," *Forbes*, July 22, 2013, www.forbes.com/sites/jjcolao/2013/07/22/e-commerce-giant-reveals-strange-strategy-sending-customers-to-competitors/.

Not Feeling Creative? Your Role in Innovation
1. Teresa Amabile, "How To Kill Creativity," *Harvard Business Review*, September 1998, 77–87.

Unveil Your New Idea Strategically
1. Pieter C. Van den Toorn, *Stravinsky and the Rite of Spring: The Beginnings of a Musical Language* (Berkeley and Los Angeles: UC Press, 1987), 6.

Communication, Collaboration & Influence
Full-Bodied Listening
1. Source: Personnel Decisions International survey of more than 4,000 U.S. managers across various industries and functions, cited in Patrick Barwise and Seán Meehan, "So You Think You're a Good Listener," *Harvard Business Review*, April 2008, https://hbr.org/2008/04/so-you-think-youre-a-good-listener.

Ask, Ask, Ask: The Power of Questions
1. "The Technium: A Conversation With Kevin Kelly," *Edge*, February 3, 2014, https://edge.org/conversation/the-technium.

2. "The Fab Five," *Drucker Institute*, April 22, 2011, www.druckerinstitute.com/2011/04/the-fab-five/.

Showing Up as Your Best: The Impact of Nonverbal Communication
1. A. Mehrabian, *Silent Messages: Implicit Communication of Emotions and Attitudes* (Belmont, CA: Wadsworth, 1981), 75–80.

2. Edward T. Hall, *The Hidden Dimension* (New York, Anchor Books, 1990), 116–125.

May I Have Your Attention, Please?
1. Mehrabian, *Silent Messages*, 75–80.

2. Allan Pease and Barbara Pease, *The Definitive Book of Body Language* (New York: Bantam Books, 2004), 255.

In a World of Too Much Information, Less Is More

1. "The Incredible Shrinking Sound Bite," *Center for Media and Public Affairs*, September 28, 2000, http://cmpa.gmu.edu/wp-content/uploads/2013/10/prev_pres_elections/2000/2000.09.28.The-Incredible-Shrinking-Sound-Bite.pdf.

2. Kevin Kelly, *New Rules for the New Economy: 10 Radical Strategies For a Connected World* (New York: Penguin, 1998), 59.

Got Stage Fright?

1. Christopher Ingraham, "America's top fears: Public speaking, heights and bugs," *Washington Post*, October 30, 2014, www.washingtonpost.com/blogs/wonkblog/wp/2014/10/30/clowns-are-twice-as-scary-to-democrats-as-they-are-to-republicans/.

How to Get People to Speak Up in Meetings

1. Alex Pentland, "The New Science of Building Great Teams," *Harvard Business Review*, April 2012.

Can We Just Talk?: When to Stop Arguing and Dialogue Instead

1. Deborah Tannen, *The Argument Culture: Stopping America's War of Words* (New York: Ballantine Books, 1999).

2. Peter N. Senge, *The Fifth Discipline: The Art and Practice of the Learning Organization* (New York: Doubleday Business, 2006), 222.

3. Ibid., 226. Based on conversations with David Bohm.

How to Influence Someone

1. Pink, Daniel H., *To Sell Is Human: The Surprising Truth About Moving Others* (New York: Riverhead Books, 2012), 20-21.

Developing Teams & Talent

Your Strengths Strategy

1. Tom Rath and Barry Conchie, *Strengths Based Leadership* (New York: Gallup, 2008), 2.

2. Richard Farson, *Management of the Absurd: Paradoxes in Leadership* (New York, Simon & Schuster, 1996), 137.

The "Feeling" Factor

1. Geoff Colvin, *Humans are Underrated: What High Achievers Know that Brilliant Machines Never Will* (New York: Portfolio, 2015), 178–179, citing research by David Engel, Anita Wooley, Lisa X. Jing, Christopher F. Chabris, Thomas Malone, "Theory of Mind Predicts Collective Intelligence," Proceedings of Collective Intelligence 2014, Cambridge, Massachusetts, http://humancomputation.com/ci2014/papers/Active%20Papers%5CPaper%20106/pdf.

Appendix

2. National sample data and occupational sample studies cited in: Isabel Briggs Myers, et al., *MBTI® Manual* (Palo Alto, CA: CPP, 2003), 157–158.

3. Gerald P. Macdaid, CAPT Data Bank, 1997, Center for Applications of Psychological Type, cited in Larry Demerest, *Looking at Type™ in the Workplace* (Gainesville, FL: Center For Applications of Psychological Type, 2003), 30.

4. Briggs Myers, et al., *MBTI® Manual*, 297.

5. Ibid., 298.

6. Colvin, *Humans are Underrated*, 69, 122–125, citing research by Anita Williams Wooley, Christopher F. Chabris, Alex Pentland, Nada Hashmi, Thomas W. Malone, "Evidence for a Collective Intelligence Factor in the Performance of Human Groups," *Science*, vol. 330, October 29, 2010, 686–668, doi: 10.1126/science.1193147.

Seven Ways for Women to Come Across More Powerfully at Work
1. Katty Kay and Claire Shipman, *The Confidence Code: The Science and Art of Self-Assurance–What Women Should Know* (New York: HarperCollins, 2014), 14–21.

2. Deborah Tannen, *Talking From 9 To 5: How Women's and Men's Conversational Styles Affect Who Gets Heard, Who Gets Credit, and What Gets Done at Work* (New York: William Morrow and Company, 1994).

3. Pease, *The Definitive Book of Body Language*, 255.

4. Ibid.

5. Ibid., 42.

6. Amy Roeder, "Do women talk more than men?" *Harvard T.H. Chan School of Public Health*, July 23, 2014, www.hsph.harvard.edu/news/features/do-women-talk-more-than-men/.

7. Sheryl Sandberg and Adam Grant, "Speaking While Female," *The New York Times*, January 12, 2015, www.nytimes.com/2015/01/11/opinion/sunday/speaking-while-female.html.

8. Briggs Myers, et al., *MBTI® Manual*, 157–158, 297, 298.

Collaborative Teams: How to Make 2+2=5
1. Bruce W. Tuckman, "Developmental sequence in small groups," *Psychological Bulletin*, Volume 63, No. 6 (1965), 384–399.

Without This, You Won't Get Much Done
1. Linda K. Stroh, *Trust Rules: How to Tell the Good Guys From the Bad Guys in Work and Life* (Westport, CT: Praeger, 2007), 81–86.

Tailored Delegation
1. Gary L. Neilson and Julie Wulf, "How Many Direct Reports," *Harvard Business Review*, April 2012, https://hbr.org/2012/04/how-many-direct-reports.

Are You Dreading Performance Reviews?
1. Dan Ariely, "What makes us feel good about our work," *ted.com*, October 2002, www.ted.com/talks/dan_ariely_what_makes_us_feel_good_about_our_work/transcript?language=en.

Update Your Motivation Methods
1. Amy Adkins, "Employee Engagement in U.S. Stagnant in 2015," *Gallup*, January 13, 2016, www.gallup.com/poll/188144/employee-engagement-stagnant-2015.aspx.

2. Quoted in Julia Hanna, "Getting Down to the Business of Creativity," *Harvard Business School Working Knowledge*, May 14, 2008.

3. Daniel Pink, *Drive: The Surprising Truth About What Motivates Us* (New York: Penguin Group, 2011).

4. Amabile, "How to Kill Creativity," 77–87.

5. Mihaly Csikszentmihalyi, *Finding Flow: The Psychology of Engagement with Everyday Life* (New York: Basic Books, 1997).

Put Humor to Work
1. "Does Humor Make Ads More Effective?" Millward Brown, accessed September 12, 2015, www.millwardbrown.com/docs/default-source/china-downloads/newsletter/3-millwardbrown_knowledgepoint_humorinadvertising.pdf.

2. Zak Starnbor, "How laughing leads to learning," American Psychological Association, *Monitor on Psychology*, June 2006, www.apa.org/monitor/jun06/learning.aspx.

3. "Career Builder Study Reveals Surprising Factors That Play a Part in Determining Who Gets Hired," *CareerBuilder.com*, August 28, 2013, www.careerbuilder.com/share/aboutus/pressreleasesdetail.aspx?sd=8/28/2013&id=pr778&ed=12/31/2013.

4. Fabio Sala, "Laughing All the Way to the Bank," *Harvard Business Review*, September 2003, https://hbr.org/2003/09/laughing-all-the-way-to-the-bank.

5. "Stress relief from laughter? It's no joke," *Mayo Clinic*, www.mayoclinic.org/healthy-lifestyle/stress-management/in-depth/stress-relief/art-20044456?pg=1.

6. Moses Ma, "The Power of Humor in Ideation and Creativity," *Psychology Today*, June 16, 2014, www.psychologytoday.com/blog/the-tao-innovation/201406/the-power-humor-in-ideation-and-creativity.

7. Tannen, *Talking From 9 To 5*, 72–76.

Bibliography

Ailes, Roger. *You Are the Message*. New York: Doubleday, 1988.

Amabile, Teresa. "How to Kill Creativity." *Harvard Business Review*, September 1998, 77–87.

Ariely, Daniel. *Predictably Irrational: The Hidden Forces That Shape Our Decisions*. New York: HarperCollins, 2010.

Bardwick, Judith. *Danger in the Comfort Zone: From Boardroom to Mailroom–How to Break the Entitlement Habit That's Killing American Business*. New York: AMACOM, 1995.

Bennis, Warren and Patricia Ward Biedermann. *Organizing Genius: The Secrets of Creative Collaboration*. New York: Basic, 1998.

Bridges, William. *Transitions: Making Sense of Life's Changes*. New York: Perseus, 1980.

Briggs Myers, Isabel. *Gifts Differing: Understanding Personality Type*. Mountain View, CA: CPP, 1995.

Briggs Myers, Isabel, Mary H. McCaulley, Naomi L. Quenk, and Allen L. Hammer. *MBTI® Manual*. Palo Alto, CA: CPP, 2003.

Carr, Nicholas. *The Shallows: What the Internet is Doing to Our Brains*. New York: Norton, 2011.

Carter, Judy. *Stand-Up Comedy: The Book*. New York: Dell, 1989.

Cialdini, Robert B. *Influence: The Psychology of Persuasion*. New York: Harper Business, 2006.

Clifton, Jim. *The Coming Jobs War*. New York: Gallup, 2011.

Appendix

Colvin, Geoff. *Humans are Underrated: What High Achievers Know that Brilliant Machines Never Will.* New York: Portfolio, 2015.

Cooperrider, David and Diana Whitney. *Appreciative Inquiry: A Positive Revolution in Change.* San Francisco: Berrett-Koehler, 2005.

Coyle, Daniel. *The Talent Code: Greatness Isn't Born. It's Grown. Here's How.* New York: Bantam, 2009.

Csikszentmihali, Mihaly. *Finding Flow: The Psychology of Engagement with Everyday Life.* New York: Basic, 1997.

de Bono, Edward. *De Bono's Thinking Course.* New York: Facts on File, 1994.

de Bono, Edward. *Six Thinking Hats.* New York: Back Bay, 1999.

Demerest, Larry. *Looking at Type™ in the Workplace.* Gainesville, FL: Center For Applications of Psychological Type, 2003.

Doyle, Michael and David Strauss. *How to Make Meetings Work.* New York: Berkley, 1993.

Farson, Richard. *Management of the Absurd: Paradoxes in Leadership.* New York, Simon & Schuster, 1996.

Florida, Richard. *Rise of the Creative Class.* New York: Basic, 2002.

Friedman, Thomas L. *The World is Flat: A Brief History of the Twenty-first Century.* New York: Farrar, Straus & Giroux, 2005.

Gallwey, W. Timothy. *The Inner Game of Work.* New York: Random House, 2001.

Gardner, John. *Intelligence Reframed: Multiple Intelligences for the 21st Century.* New York: Basic, 2000.

Glasser, William. *Control Theory: An Explanation of How We Control Our Lives.* New York: Harper, 1985.

Glickstein, Lee. *Be Heard Now!* New York: Broadway, 1999.

Goldsmith, Marshall. *What Got You Here Won't Get You There: How Successful People Become Even More Successful.* New York: Hyperion, 2007.

Gostick, Adrian and Scott Christopher. *The Levity Effect: Why It Pays to Lighten Up.* Hoboken, NJ: Wiley, 2008.

Handy, Charles. *The Age of Unreason*. Boston: Harvard Business School Press, 1990.

Heim, Pat and Susan Murphy. *In the Company of Women: Turning Workplace Conflict into Powerful Alliances*. New York: Tarcher, 2001.

Herzberg, Frederick. "One More Time: How Do You Motivate Employees?" *Harvard Business Review*, September–October, 1987.

Isaacs, William. *Dialogue and the Art of Thinking Together*. New York: Doubleday, 1999.

Johansson, Frans. *The Medici Effect: Breakthrough Insights at the Intersection of Ideas, Concepts, & Cultures*. Boston: Harvard Business Review Press, 2003.

Kaplan, Jerry. *Humans Need Not Apply: A Guide to Wealth and Work in the Age of Artificial Intelligence*. New Haven: Yale University Press, 2015.

Katzenbach, Jon R. and Douglas K. Smith. *The Wisdom of Teams: Creating the High Performance Organization*. New York: Harper Business, 2003.

Kay, Katty and Claire Shipman. *The Confidence Code: The Science and Art of Self-Assurance–What Women Should Know*. New York: HarperCollins, 2014.

Kelley, Tom. *The Art of Innovation: Lessons in Creativity from IDEO, America's Leading Design Firm*. New York: Crown Business, 2001.

Kelly, Kevin. *New Rules for the New Economy: 10 Radical Strategies For a Connected World*. New York: Penguin, 1998.

Kidder, Rushworth. *How Good People Make Tough Choices: Resolving the Dilemmas of Ethical Living*. New York: Morrow, 1995.

Kotter, John. *Leading Change*. Boston, Harvard Business, 1996.

Kouzes, James M. and Barry Z. Posner. *The Leadership Challenge*. San Francisco: Jossey-Bass, 2002.

Kouzes, James M. and Barry Z. Posner. *The Truth About Leadership*. San Francisco: Jossey-Bass, 2010.

Lemov, Doug. *Practice Perfect: 42 Rules for Getting Better at Getting Better*. San Francisco: Jossey-Bass, 2012.

Lencioni, Patrick. *The Five Dysfunctions of a Team: A Leadership Fable*. San Francisco: Jossey-Bass, 2002.

Luntz, Frank. *Words That Work: It's Not What You Say, It's What People Hear*. New York: Hyperion, 2007.

Mackenzie, Alec and Pat Nickerson. *The Time Trap: The Classic Book on Time Management*. New York: AMACON, 2007.

Mapes, James. *Quantum Leap Thinking: An Owner's Guide to the Mind*. Naperville, IL: Sourcebooks, 2003.

Maruska, Don. *How Great Decisions Get Made: 10 Easy Steps to Get Agreement on Even the Toughest Issues*. New York: AMACOM, 2006.

Morgenstern, Julie. *Time Management from the Inside Out*. New York: Holt, 2004.

Osborn, Alex. *Applied Imagination: Principles and Procedures of Creative Problem-Solving*. New York: Scribner, 1963.

Pease, Allan and Barbara Pease. *The Definitive Book of Body Language*. New York: Bantam, 2004.

Pentland, Alex. "The New Science of Building Great Teams." *Harvard Business Review*, April 2012.

Pink, Daniel: *Drive: The Surprising Truth About What Motivates Us*. New York: Penguin Group, 2011.

Pink, Daniel. *A Whole New Mind: Why Right-Brainers Will Rule the Future*. New York: Berkley, 2006.

Quinn, Carol. *Don't Hire Anyone Without Me*. Orlando: HABooks, 2002.

Rath, Tom and Barry Conchie. *Strengths Based Leadership*. New York: Gallup, 2008.

Rees, Fran. *The Facilitator Excellence Handbook*. San Francisco: Pfeiffer, 2005.

Ressler, Cali and Jody Thompson. *Why Work Sucks and How to Fix It: The Results-Only Revolution*. New York: Penguin, 2008.

Rock, David. *Your Brain at Work: Strategies For Overcoming Distraction, Regaining Focus and Working Smarter All Day Long*. New York, HarperCollins, 2009.

Rose, Colin. *Accelerated Learning*. Niles, IL: Nightingale-Conant, 1995.

Seligman, Martin E. P. *Flourish: A Visionary New Understanding of Happiness and Well-being*. New York: Free Press, 2011.

Senge, Peter. *The Fifth Discipline: The Art & Practice of The Learning Organization.* New York: Doubleday Business, 2006.

Snow, Shane. *Smartcuts: How Hackers, Innovators, and Icons Accelerate Success.* New York: HarperCollins, 2014.

Stavros, Jackie, David Cooperrider and Lynn Kelley. "Strategic Inquiry > Appreciative Intent: Inspiration to SOAR." *AI Practitioner,* November 2003.

Stroh, Linda K. *Trust Rules: How to Tell the Good Guys From the Bad Guys in Work and Life.* Westport, CT: Praeger, 2007.

Tannen, Deborah. *The Argument Culture: Stopping America's War of Words.* New York: Ballantine, 1999.

Tannen, Deborah. *Talking From 9 To 5: How Women's and Men's Conversational Styles Affect Who Gets Heard, Who Gets Credit, and What Gets Done at Work.* New York: Morrow, 1994.

Tracy, Brian. *Eat That Frog: 21 Great Ways to Stop Procrastinating and Get More Done in Less Time.* San Francisco: Berrett-Koehler, 2007.

Van Gundy, Arthur. *101 Activities for Teaching Creativity and Problem-Solving.* San Francisco: Pfeiffer, 2004.

Wheatley, Margaret. *Turning to One Another: Simple Conversations to Restore Hope to the Future.* San Francisco: Berrett-Kohler, 2009.

Wilder, Lilyan. *Professionally Speaking.* New York: Simon & Schuster, 1986.

About The Author

Jane Moyer blends her experience in executive-level management, sales and marketing, career coaching, and the performing arts to bring potential to life.

Rising from coordinator to Senior Vice President during her 25-year career at Home Box Office, Jane experienced firsthand the challenges of producing results month after month, developing teams and talent, navigating large and small organizations, adapting to change, and facing skeptics when innovating, all while balancing career, travel, and family. She learned from watching diverse leaders among her clients and colleagues, from first-rate coaches and mentors, and by experimenting, adapting, and making plenty of her own mistakes out in the real world.

Since founding New Century Leadership LLC in 2005, Jane has focused on bringing out the best in other leaders. She supplemented her corporate experience with advanced coaching training, certification on leadership development assessments such as MBTI®, and extensive research on leadership topics, workplace best practices, and economic trends. With this combination, she guides clients in developing high-impact skills, honing individual leadership styles, and sniffing out opportunity to create vibrant futures.

Additionally, her lifelong passion for the performing arts contributes to her flair for creativity, talent development, and connection with audiences. She draws on her experience performing, arranging, and teaching music to help leaders develop effective style and achieve excellence, both as individual performers and as collaborators.

Jane earned both her Bachelors and Masters degrees at Michigan State University. She's always been intrigued by pioneers, futurists, communicators, comedians, and creatives.

She's deeply grateful for the support of her family, her friends and teachers, and those who have given her the opportunity to develop and use her craft.

Visit Jane at www.LeadersLab.com. To book workshops, talks, or coaching, write to her at Jane@LeadersLab.com.

Made in the USA
Lexington, KY
30 September 2018